Globalisation and
the International Economy

Michael Hedegaard

Globalisation and the International Economy

Djøf Publishing
Copenhagen 2018

Michael Hedegaard
Globalisation and the International Economy

1th edition

© 2018 by Djøf Publishing
Djøf Forlag

Cover: Mette Schou, gipsy graphics
Print: Toptryk, Gråsten

Printed in Denmark 2018
ISBN 978-87-574-3974-8

Sold and distributed in Scandinavia by:
DJØF Publishing
Copenhagen, Denmark
Email: forlag@djoef.dk
www.djoef-forlag.dk

Sold and distributed in North America by:
International Specialized Book Services (ISBS)
Portland, USA
Email: orders@isbs.com
www.isbs.com

Sold in all other countries by:
The Oxford Publicity Partnership Ltd
Towcester, UK
Email: djof@oppuk.co.uk
www.oppuk.co.uk

Distributed in all other countries by:
Marston Book Services
Abingdon, Oxon, UK
Email: trade.orders@marston.co.uk
www.marston.co.uk

Contents

Acknowledgements

My sincere gratitude goes to my two children, Maja and Oskar, and to my friend and fellow teacher, assistant professor Mikkel Godt Gregersen at Copenhagen Business School (CBS), who is the author of Chapter 2 on trade theories. Without his capable assistance this book would not have been written. My thanks also go to my longstanding friend, John Sanders, who added much value with his insights and transformed my non-native English into smoother flowing prose while still retaining my thoughts and ideas. Deep appreciation is also extended to the Programme Director at DIS, Susanne Goul Hovmand, for enthusiastically backing this project all the way from concept to publication. Thanks, too, are in order to the many other contributors to this book, in particular associate professor Edward Ashbee at CBS; economic and business commentator Leif Beck Fallesen; Director Jørn Fredsgaard Sørensen at Eksport Kredit Fonden EKF; macroeconomist Søren Vestergaard from Sydbank; associate professor Michael Wendelboe Hansen, and Ph.D. fellow Henrik Gundelach, both from CBS. Last but not least, I wish to convey my heartfelt appreciation to Jeppe Strandsbjerg at Djøf for making this book possible.

Copenhagen, July 2018
Michael Hedegaard

Introduction

This book is the result of countless classroom hours teaching global economics to American university students and meeting people from around the world who experience globalisation first-hand. The students were particularly inspiring because our discussions often went beyond the economic models to reflect on globalisation within its historical, cultural, political, and social contexts. The technicalities of the models became less relevant in these moments, but understanding their key concepts was vital to grasping the implications of globalisation's developments.

The global economy never ceases to fascinate and surprise as its many facets evolve at an ever-increasing rate. This book introduces global economics in its historical setting and combines this understanding with real life examples. Along the way, the book considers a variety of topics such as financial globalisation, unbundling of tasks, global value chains, protectionism, the nation-state, and resistance to globalisation.

This book stems from a desire to have a textbook which provides an overview of key economic models and theories which both aid in understanding today's global economy and offer a basis for reflection and discussion. It has a distinct economics perspective without being overly theoretical or technical precisely because a practical, user-friendly style is its goal. It is meant as a tool to inspire discussion and analysis of the global economy.

The first part of *Globalisation and the International Economy* contains four chapters on globalisation, trade models, tariffs and protectionism, and lastly financial globalisation. These intriguing topics are central to a study of global economics. The second part contains a collection of insightful contributions from experts on specialised topics which are relevant in today's globalized economy. The first article discusses the current de-globalising processes and politics seen around the world. Related to this follows an article which analyses and takes stock of the status of one of the most ambitious political and economic integration projects of our time, namely the European Union. The next article explains export finance and offers insights into country risk and how export finance works in practice. Next follows a practical example of how the free movement of labour within the European Union has direct effect on the Danish labour market. Finally, the last article discusses the nature and implications of the growing stream of foreign direct investments into emerging markets.

It is my hope that this book will be valuable not only to economists and students, but also to members of the general public who have an interest in globalisation and its impact on the international economy. If it can shed any light on the drivers and inherent challenges of globalisation, it will have accomplished its goal.

CHAPTER 1

Globalisation

Globalisation is a phenomenon that impacts people, countries, cultures, economies, politics and companies in important ways. In this book we focus on globalisation from the Industrial Revolution onwards, i.e., beginning from the 18th century to the present day. However, globalisation is not merely a modern phenomenon: it took place during the Bronze Age over 4,000 years ago as trade routes along European rivers enabled the travel of people and goods across traditional boundaries. Bronze tools from the Mediterranean were exchanged for amber from Scandinavia and blue glass pearls from Ancient Egypt were worn by Jutland women as highly prized adornments. Meanwhile, the tin used for making bronze in Europe came all the way from modern-day Afghanistan.

As centuries passed, international trade continued with ebbs and flows. In the second century BCE though, globalisation surged as China established the Silk Road across Asia and the Middle East to facilitate its lucrative silk trade. This trade lasted for 1,500 years, forever altering the face of this vast region as cultures, languages, and religions were widely interchanged. In the early to middle portion of this period the Roman Empire connected Europe to this network, using its military might and maritime power to expand the spice trade from India and Arabia. The net result of both globalisation eras is that an increased flow of people, goods, and capital resulted in an exchange of ideas across cultures which gave countless millions the insights of a perspective far beyond their own.

The globalisation of the 21st century shares many of these same characteristics, yet it is also markedly different. This difference is often described as one of intensity and scope, not least because of the speed at which information travels thanks to the advances of technology we take for granted such as email, the internet, and social media. Other differentiating factors in modern globalisation are the weight of services in the world economy and the vast range of products and services that is traded. A generation ago things like call centres, bookkeeping, and payroll operations were considered non-tradable, but with the advent of simplified communication across long distances, the outsourcing of these and countless other services has become commonplace and even birthed new industries. Nor has manufacturing been exempt from outsourcing, as cheaper labour costs and economical maritime transport create incentives for multinational corporations to shift locations when desired.

These issues lead to important questions. Will an increasingly globalised and inter-connected world allow corporations to spread across the globe with each business sector operating where it is most efficient to do so? Or will steadily rising labour costs in developing countries catalyse the return of manufacturing and mid-level skilled jobs to the traditional industrialised economies in a way that consolidates the corporate structure? In many parts of the world, both the backlash against globalisation and the increase in nationalism is reversing this trend altogether - so perhaps neither of these things will happen.

This book endeavours to provide a framework for developing reflections and answers to these questions as it explores the drivers and consequences of globalisation in the international economy both historically and today. We start by defining globalisation and discussing its two most recent waves. Then we consider the interdependence and role of nation-states, as well as global value chains, wealth and income distribution, and the differences in how institutions are established and designed to function in different nations.

1.1   Defining and Understanding Globalisation

Virtually all nations today are highly interdependent in the sense that goods and services, people, and capital are permitted to move across borders. This interdependence has many impacts, including such elements as national income and consumption, business development, technology, wages, and politics. People around the world today are more likely than ever to buy foreign goods and services, study abroad, visit other countries, have overseas investments or work for a company owned by foreign investors. The term globalisation began to be used more commonly during the 1980s and most would agree that today's world is highly globalised. In the following sections we will delve into the implications of this term.

Defining the degree of globalisation which exists around the world is not a clear-cut task. Starting broadly, in 1990 sociologist Anthony Giddens in his book *The Consequences of Modernity* defined globalisation as, *'the intensification of worldwide social relations which link distant localities in such a way that local happenings are shaped by events occurring many miles away and vice versa'*.

In the following sections we will pursue an economics perspective on globalisation. One classical way of measuring the openness, or globalisation, of a nation's economy is to calculate the proportion of exports and imports relative to GDP. This reflects the degree to which its national output is dedicated to production of goods for export and the quantity of products it consumes from abroad.

The following chart displays the level of openness in the world economy by considering global trade (imports plus exports) as a percentage of GDP from 1960 to 2016. It clearly illustrates the way in which trade has expanded at a much greater pace than GDP over the period, which indicates increasing globalisation.

Figure 1. World Trade as Percentage of World GDP

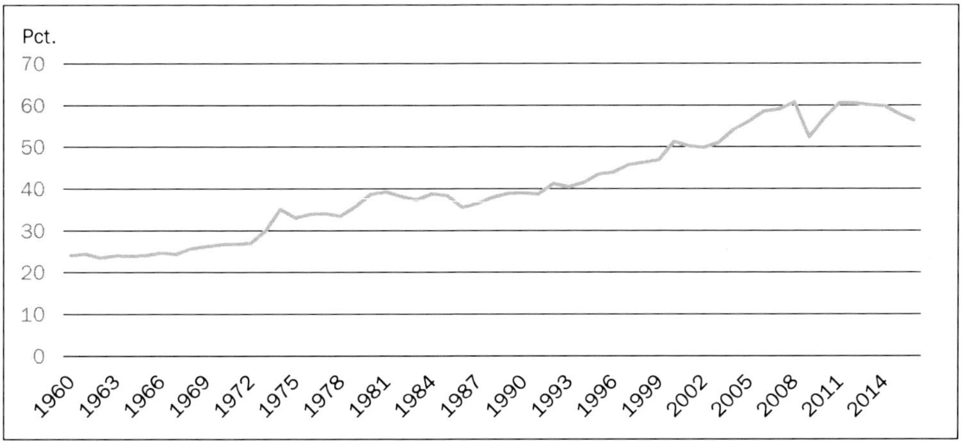

Sources: World Bank and OECD

The chart shows there were several periods of flat to negative growth in global trade over the previous decades. Of special note is the plunge in trade in the wake of the 2008 global financial crisis and the strong recovery followed in recent years by a gradual decline.

The median openness in global trade chart above masks significant differences among the world's nations. The following chart drills down further by showing the openness of four different countries – Ghana, the United States, Denmark, and China. Each country's degree of openness, as measured by trade as a percentage of GDP increased from 1960 to 2016, but at different rates and along different individual paths.

Figure 2. Trade as Percentage of GDP

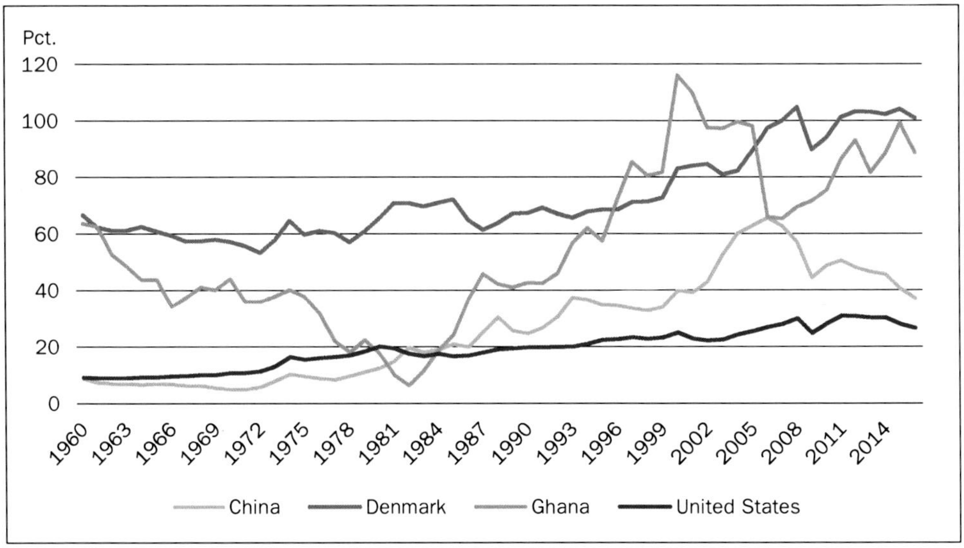

Sources: World Bank and OECD

A 2016 snapshot of trade as a percentage of GDP for a wider selection of countries underscores the significant variations which exist around the globe:

Table 1.

Country	Trade as % of 2016 GDP
Netherlands	154 %
Denmark	101 %
France	61 %
Russia	46 %
India	40 %
United States	27 %
Brazil	25 %

Sources: World Bank and OECD

We can derive at least two important insights from these inter-country data:

1. Smaller countries tend to be more open to global trade than larger ones because their domestic production possibilities are more limited and cannot supply as wide a range of goods and services.
2. Trade as a general concept veils the significant variations between countries. This is because some countries – like Russia or Ghana – primarily export commodities

like crude oil or agricultural products, whereas others, like the United States, have a well-diversified export/import portfolio of manufactured goods and services.

In addition to openness to trade, globalisation is concerned with the flow of capital around the world. As seen in the chart below, the stock of global foreign investment liabilities has increased significantly since the 1990s but remained relatively stable since the 2008 global financial crisis. It is clear from these data that capital is significantly more global today than it was some 20 years ago.

Figure 3. Gross stock of foreign investment liabilities, USD trillion at annual (nominal) exchange rates

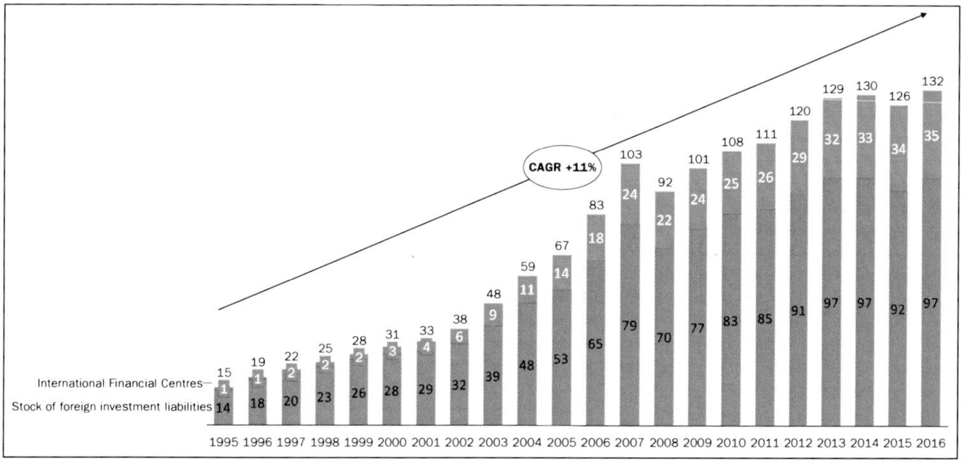

Source: McKinsey Global Institute

If we zero in specifically on the trend for Foreign Direct Investments[1] (FDI) as a percentage of GDP we see a pattern (Figure 4) emerge where FDI gained momentum during the 1990s up to the 2008 global financial crisis, then dropped sharply, but has since recovered and remained stable.

An example of a broader measure of globalisation is the well-regarded KOF Globalisation Index developed by the Swiss research institution ETH Zürich. It measures the economic, social, and political dimensions of globalisation on the basis of quantitative data. Using 23 variables, the KOF Globalisation Index covers 187 countries beginning from 1970 and ranks them on a scale from 1 to 100.

1. An investment is generally considered a Foreign Direct Investment (FDI) if a foreign-based company or individual holds 10 percent or more of a domestic company's stock (OECD).

Figure 4. Foreign Direct Investment net inflow as Percentage of GDP

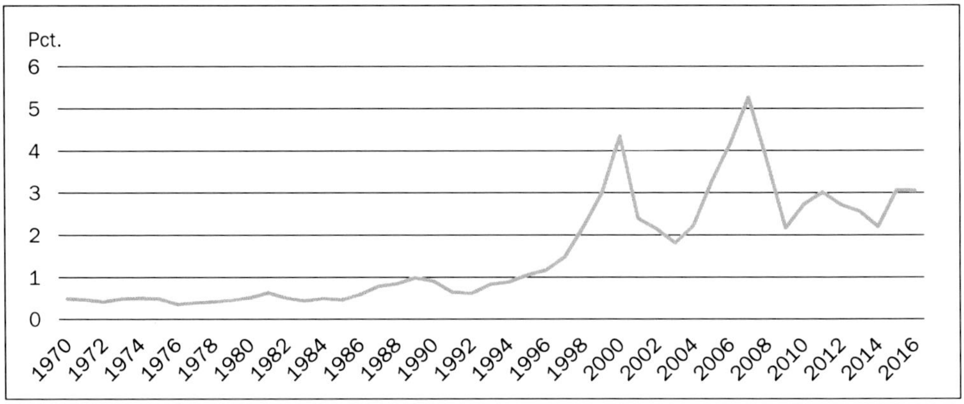

Source: World Bank

The *economic dimension* of globalisation reflects the extent of cross-border trade, investment, and revenue flows in relation to GDP, as well as the impact of restrictions on trade and capital transactions.

The *social dimension* of globalisation is measured in three ways: First, it considers cross-border personal contacts in the form of telephone calls, letters, and tourist visits, as well as the number of foreigners resident in the country. Second, cross-border information flows are measured in terms of access to the internet, television, and foreign media outlets. Finally, the index evaluates cultural proximity to the global mainstream by quantifying the number of McDonald's and IKEA branches, as well as book imports and exports in relation to GDP.

The *political dimension* of globalisation is measured in terms of the number of foreign embassies located in a country, how many international organisations it belongs to, how many UN peace-keeping missions it has participated in, and the amount of bilateral and multilateral agreements it has concluded since 1945.

The following chart shows the KOF Index of Globalisation with data through 2015. Historically, globalisation has risen steadily, but in 2015, it decreased for the first time since the 1970s. The fall was due to a decline in economic globalisation, with social globalisation stagnating and political globalisation increasing slightly.

Interestingly, eight out of the ten most globalised countries are small European countries – The Netherlands, Switzerland, Sweden, Austria, Belgium, Denmark, France, Germany, Finland, and Norway.

Figure 5. Index of Globalisation Worldwide

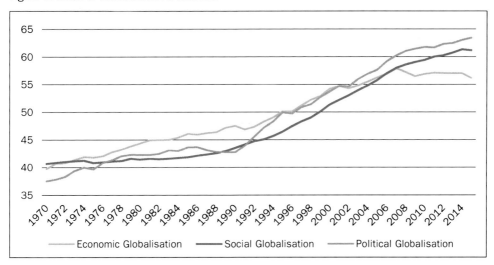

Source: KOF Globalisation Index, ETH

What is it that drives economies towards globalisation? In the following sections we discuss two key perspectives on this question. The first, as presented by Canadian economist Michael D. Bordo, emphasises **technology and economics**; the second, by Oxford economist and historian Kevin O'Rourke, considers **politics and hegemonic power**. These discussions consider two distinct periods of modern globalisation; the first from 1870 to 1914 and the second wave from the late 1940s onwards.

1.2   Economic Perspective on Globalisation

Bordo (2002) views globalisation primarily as an economic phenomenon which is driven by developments in the **trade of goods and services, the movement of people and labour, and the movement of capital**. If we focus on the first period of globalisation in the modern era, from circa 1870 to 1914, we see that a significant increase in trade was driven by the absence of war, an exchange rate stability given by the gold standard, and a sharp reduction in transportation costs thanks to breakthroughs such as the advent of trans-ocean steamships and the opening of the Suez Canal. During this time the mobility of people was very high, with few restrictions on immigration, and capital flows were massive as the core countries of Europe invested in their colonies at the periphery of the world and received commodities in return.

Ultimately, this expansion of nearly half a century came to a halt due to the imposition of capital controls and the onset of World War I.

The main difference between capital flows of 100 to 150 years ago and today is that present-day lenders and borrowers possess a depth and variety of finance options which their counterparts could never have imagined. Different, too, is the increase in portfolio capital flows among financial institutions – that is, capital flows which are not directly linked to economic trade but rather to portfolio investments in stocks, bonds, and other financial instruments which are not considered foreign direct investment. These investments are often referred to as 'hot money', which we will discuss in Chapter 4 when we deal with global finance.

The inhabitant of London could order by telephone, sipping his morning coffee in bed, the various products of the whole earth, in such quantity as he might see fit, and reasonably expect their early delivery upon his doorstep; he could at the same moment and by the same means adventure his wealth in the natural resources and new enterprises in any quarter of the world, and share, without exertion or even trouble, in their prospective fruits and advantages; or he could decide to couple the security of his fortunes with the good faith of the townspeople of any substantial municipality in any continent that fancy or information might recommend. He could secure forthwith, if he wished it, cheap and comfortable means of transit to any country or climate without passport or other formality.

J.M. Keynes, *The Economic Consequences of the Peace*

All old-established national industries have been destroyed or are daily being destroyed. They are dislodged by new industries, whose introduction becomes a life and death question for all civilized nations, by industries that no longer work up indigenous raw material, but raw material drawn from the remotest zones; industries whose products are consumed, not only at home, but in every quarter of the globe. In place of the old wants, satisfied by the productions of the country, we find new wants, requiring for their satisfaction the products of distant lands and climes. In place of old local and national seclusion and self-sufficiency, we have intercourse in every direction, universal inter-dependency of nations.

K. Marx and F. Engels, The Communist Manifesto, 1850, repr.
in *Marx and Engels Selected Works*, London: Lawrence & Wishart, 1968, p. 39

Classical macroeconomic theory dictates that the free flow of goods, services, people, and capital should gradually cause prices to converge. If a good can be traded just as freely in Pennsylvania as in Portugal, competition should cause prices to align so that the only differences are those that reflect local costs, such as transportation, warehousing, and similar geographical considerations.

The free flow of economic inputs during this first wave of globalisation caused prices to converge between the United States and Europe. Wages fell in the U.S. as a large influx of workers competed for jobs, but in Europe they increased as the labour force contracted. Consequently, investors saw their return on capital – or rent – increase in the United States but decrease in Europe. With wages rising and rent falling in Europe, the overall level of financial inequality decreased, whereas it increased in the United States as the reverse dynamic played out. The net result was that capital owners in Europe saw their lot worsen, so they argued for higher tariffs to protect their interests against the import of cheaper goods; American workers, on the other hand, saw their wages decline and argued for curbs to immigration. We see through this example that globalisation has winners and losers, but who they are depends on globalisation's impact in a particular location. This, in turn, has consequences for income distribution and inequality. One lesson from the past is therefore that one of the inherent risks of a globalisation-driven price convergence is that it can foment political backlash in the form of protectionism, tariffs, immigration policies, and capital controls. This has direct relevance to our world today.

During this period of expanding globalisation the worldwide monetary system had the gold standard as its backbone: key industrial powers had agreed to hold their currencies at fixed exchange rates relative to one another and at a rate redeemable for gold. This eliminated most foreign exchange risk, which in turn provided the necessary stability for trade. It also restrained global monetary policy because a nation cannot expand or contract its money supply independently if its currency is fixed to a peg and capital flows freely. A severe test, however, came in 1914 as World War I erupted across Europe. Great Britain broke its peg to gold in order to print pound sterling in any amount the war effort might demand. Other countries followed suit, and the standard was abandoned for the war's duration. Inflation soared with uncontrolled money printing, most famously in Germany's Weimar Republic, and sovereign debt levels skyrocketed. Meanwhile, capital controls became commonplace as governments sought to stem the convertibility of devalued currency units into gold. These impacts continued unabated until 1925 when Great Britain re-instituted the gold standard on a limited basis. Many countries followed its lead, which helped to stabilise prices, but this tightening of the global money supply ultimately led to deflation as fewer dollars, pounds sterling, and French francs, for example, were available to purchase the ever-expanding supply of goods created by the Roaring Twenties' post-war economic recovery. Things finally came to head in 1929 as the Great Stock Market Crash in the United States ushered in the Great Depression. The gold standard was abandoned for most purposes four years later, in 1933, at the London Economic Conference when U.S. President Franklin D. Roosevelt declined to stabilise world currencies by letting the dollar rise against them so that other nations' dollar-denominated debts would be diminished in real terms. This action undermined the international monetary system at the height of the Great Depression and led to severe capital controls. This restriction on the movement of capital situation remained largely unchanged for over 40 years, until the 1970s when they were finally lifted and floating exchange rates gradually became the norm.

GOLD STANDARD AND IMPOSSIBILITY TRIANGLE

The gold standard which existed from the 1800s to the early 1900s was characterised by each nation's money supply consisting of gold or paper money redeemable into gold (backed by gold reserves). Each nation set the official price of its national currency in terms of a gold equivalent and would buy or sell gold at that price. Gold would also be freely traded. With this structure monetary policy and currency prices would be inextricably linked to the amount of gold a country accumulated as reserves. If the current account was positive, the nation would increase its stock of gold and thus its money supply; conversely, a deficit country would see its money supply decrease because of an outflow of gold. In practice, this meant a fixed exchange rate system.

'In my view the whole management of the domestic economy depends upon being free to have the appropriate rate of interest without reference to rates prevailing elsewhere in the world. Capital control is a corollary to this.'

Keynes, *Collected Works*, Vol. XXV, p. 149

Michael D. Bordo's perspective is that economic factors are the primary catalyst for free-flowing goods and services, labour, and capital, and that this is the driver of globalisation.

1.3   Political Perspective on Globalisation

We now shift our focus to the political and hegemonic aspects of globalisation. As stated previously, O'Rourke (2009) sees globalisation as closely linked to politics: the more in favour of international trade the world's political consensus may be, the more globalisation will advance. A corollary, though, is that globalisation can be easily reversed if the political winds begin to change. O'Rourke argues that the intensity of global trade depends on the total costs of trading, which then include both explicit economic costs such as transportation and tariffs as emphasised by Bordo and the implicit costs influenced by political factors. A favourable political environment can reduce implicit costs, while an unfavourable climate can increase them.

During the wave of globalisation which began in the 1800s, Great Britain held geo-political hegemony across the world. Its power was recognised in the old adage, 'The sun never sets on the British empire,' and indeed it never did. From Africa to India, in Asia and the Middle East, the island kingdom held sway. One consequence was that Great Britain sought to reduce the implicit political costs of trading and therefore promoted globalisation through its laws. One key instance was the abolition of the Corn Laws in 1846 whereby trade in food and grain ('corn') was liberalised. That this period coincided with industrialisation only reinforced and accelerated the economic growth of the rapidly industrialising countries in Western Europe and North America, which in turn cemented their status as elite world powers. Consequently, this period saw globalisation promoted both by technological advances such as the steamboat, railroads, the telegraph, radio, and factories, and by geopolitical forces. Urbanisation, economic specialisation, and the application of economies of scale became heavily concentrated in these countries, thereby leading to enormous income divergences between industrialised countries and the rest of the world. This period of globalisation was characterised by low regulation of immigration, free trade, limited controls on capital flows, and exchange rates governed by the gold standard. As noted previously, however, this came to a sudden and complete halt with the outbreak of World War I in 1914 – i.e., it was political in nature. Similarly, the de-globalisation which accompanied the Great Depression was not grounded in a cessation of technological progress but rather stemmed from overly protectionist policies.

Global trade up to World War I was dominated by Europe (and European colonies) and the United States as seen in the table below.

Table. 2. Top Trading Nations – Exports in USD (millions)

1865		1913	
United Kingdom	11,816	United Kingdom	44,152
Germany	6,699	Germany	42,016
Belgium	5,368	South Africa	25,238
India	4,864	United States	21,277
France	4,513	France	14,158
Russia	3,429	India	13,890
China	2,750	Russia	10,066
United States	2,152	Belgium	8,731
Netherlands	2,145	Switzerland	7,937
Italy	1,688	Australia	6,860

Source: Maddison, Oxford economics. Numbers in 2010 prices and exchange rates

'I sympathise ... with those who would minimise, rather than ... maximise, economic entanglement between nations. Ideas, knowledge, art hospitality, travel – these are the things which should of their nature be international. But let goods be homespun whenever it is reasonably and conveniently possible; and above all let finance be primarily national.'

John Maynard Keynes, 1933, *National Self Sufficiency*

The second wave of globalisation began in the aftermath of World War II. Reconstruction of a global world order was led primarily by the United States, backed by Western Europe, and facilitated through a number of supra-national institutions that promoted cross-border cooperation in trade, finance, and technology. Key examples included the United Nations (UN), International Monetary Fund (IMF), World Bank (WB), the General Agreement on Tariffs and Trade (GATT), and the Bretton Woods agreement of 1944. From 1945 to 1973 there were significant reductions in tariffs, particularly for manufactured goods between developed countries, but other barriers to trade remained in force as legacy policies dating from the Great Depression. These included barriers to immigration, strict capital controls, and an exchange rate regime where gold was fixed at $ 35 per ounce, with all other currencies convertible into dollars. Consequently, during this period globalisation was primarily focused on trade liberalisation, and much less on capital liberalisation and the free movement of labour. In fact, the International Monetary Fund, which was established as part of the Bretton Woods agreement, was tasked specifically with stabilising global financial flows and exchange rates through the gold standard and providing capital to developing countries. This perspective was due in no small measure to the lingering memory of soaring post-World War I inflation and the Great Depression, which held that floating exchange rates were a source of instability and detrimental to the promotion of free trade.

In fact, problems arose in the 1970s with the Bretton Woods system because the United States, as the owner of the reserve currency of the world, ran balance-of-payment deficits. In short, the U.S. imported more goods than it exported, which had the effect of sending dollars abroad. Put another way, the United States accumulated foreign liabilities to countries holding dollars and was forced to deplete its stocks of gold as these countries' central banks converted dollars into gold at the $35 rate. As a result, whereas the United States began the Bretton Woods period holding 75% of the world's gold stock, by the mid-1960s its reserves had gradually declined and its liabilities to foreign central banks exceeded its remaining supply of gold. Had these central banks tried to convert their accumulated dollar reserves into gold all at once the United States could not have met its contractual obligations. The consumption driven appetite of the world's largest economy had turned the United States from the largest creditor in the world into its greater debtor. Finally, in 1971, pressed by gold convertibility concerns and wanting to fund U.S. involvement in the Vietnam War by printing dollars without restriction, President Nixon closed the gold window altogether. This was the death knell for the Bretton Woods agreement, and in 1974 exchange rates floated freely on the world markets for the first time in over forty years.

Table 3. The Mundell-Fleming trilernma: three possible monetary orders

Policy Choices	Gold Standard	Bretton Woods	1971/75 on
Fixed Exchange Rates	**Yes** fixed against gold	**Yes** fixed vs $ $ fixed vs gold	**No** floating rates (many LDCs –pegs) (EU – an internal peg via ERM/EMS)
Capital Mobility	**Yes** but few instruments	**No** capital controls in Europe, Japan	**Yes** many instruments
Monetary Policy	**No** few central banks; but Bank of England could move system	**Yes** central banks manipulate money supply; governments provide credit	**Yes** weak, operates indirectly through exchange rate

At the same time that Bretton Woods was collapsing, free trade was expanding and multinational corporations (MNCs) began to dominate the global landscape. Capital started to flow en masse as controls were eased, transportation costs decreased with the advent of container shipping, and the meteoric rise of information and communication technology quickly gathered force. This period also saw the creation of the European Economic Community (EEC), now called the European Union (EU), which provided an internal free market for Europe and later a common currency, the euro. In the eyes of many people, this second wave of globalisation, though it began after the end World War II, only truly began in earnest during the 1970s.

O'Rourke's perspective is that politics play a determining role in how globalisation is carried out, and that it is the strongest political nations, or hegemons, which have the power to influence its direction and pace.

1.4   Hegemonic Stability

The two waves of globalisation before and after the world wars seem to indicate that the dominant influence of first Great Britain and then the United States, in conjunction with their willingness to promote free trade, were fundamental to the advance of globalisation. This assumption forms the basis of the Hegemonic Stability Theory (HST). According to this theory, an open international economic system should be presided over by a single state with a dominant position, and the global political economy should be determined by the distribution of power and influence among its leading states (Webb & Krasner 1989, cited in Broome, 2014). A hegemon is able to maintain international regimes, which then leads to stability in the world order. 'Without a hegemon, international cooperation in trade, monetary, and most other matters in international affairs becomes exceptionally difficult, if not impossible, to achieve' (Gilpin, 2001). The reason international cooperation is so challenging in the absence of a hegemon is because one state is usually needed to provide common or public goods in the form of trade liberalisation and the enforcement of treaties and alliances which other states may be unable or unwilling to provide. HST suggests that cooperation works because the hegemonic power has economic incentives to promote it and to ensure compliance by the rest of the world.

There have been theoretical criticisms of HST, the most important being that states could choose to cooperate with one another and create a liberalised international order even in the absence of a hegemonic power. However, HST argues that this will not happen in practice because the creation of a stable global economy has never occurred without a hegemonic power. Proponents of the theory argue that the liberalised post-war global economy is based on the economic and political domination of the United States (Gilpin, 2001). Some theorists have also argued that HST suggests that American power is slowly waning as other potential hegemons (i.e., China) begin to emerge and as the productivity growth of the U.S. continues its gradual decline, which began in the early 1970s. Ultimately, they postulate that this relative power decline has placed the continued existence of a liberalised world economy in danger (Gilpin, 2001).

Mancur Olson defines a hegemonic power as 'one that finds it in its own self-interest to see that various international collective goods are provided' (cited in Gilpin, 2001). He argues that when a hegemonic power becomes relatively less important in the world economy, the hegemon's incentive to continue providing international collective goods diminishes (Gilpin, 2001). In 1960, for example, the United States' GDP represented 40% of global GDP, but by the end of 2017 this contribution had declined to only 24% (World Bank). Because the relative strength of the U.S. economy is declining and now constitutes less of the world economy than before, it is argued that this has led to a resurgence of protectionist ideas and a reduction in the United States' willingness to provide foreign aid or shoulder defense treaties to the same degree as before (Gilpin, 2001). The increased amount of American protectionist policies in response to the emergence of new exporters of manufactured goods outside the United States has fomented a shift towards greater nationalism and economic regionalism.

The rebuilding of a devastated, war-torn Europe after the First and Second World Wars can be understood in large measure through a political-economic lens as well. Reconstruction efforts were economic in nature, since much of Europe's infrastructure and economic base had been destroyed and needed massive investment to begin functioning again. At the same time, however, there was a significant political component involved. Many architects of these reconstruction efforts hoped to build a better society by means of the so-called welfare state, where the citizens of a country had their economic well-being assured by the government in a way they hoped would promote a lasting peace and ensure the 'greater good'. Consequently, the nation-state as a political entity played a central role in European economies during the post-World War II wave of resurgent globalisation – interestingly at a time when this very globalisation was gradually diminishing the role of the nation-state.

As noted in Section 1.2, this immediate post-war period saw the implementation of the Bretton Woods reserve currency system and the creation of key international initiatives such as the World Bank, the IMF, and the General Agreement on Tariffs and Trade (GATT). The overarching objective in each case was to increase international trade, but in a way where individual nations retained control over their own economies, welfare systems, and monetary and fiscal policies. To illustrate this point, one result of GATT, which later came to be known as the World Trade Organization (or WTO) is that the average import tariffs for participating nations have been reduced from about 40% in 1947 to only a few percentage points today. However, trade restrictions still remain in force, particularly in regard to agricultural products (Beskrivende dansk økonomi, 2016).

Consequently, to a certain extent the Bretton Woods system can be regarded as promoting free trade but instituting capital controls in order to protect interventionist welfare states from the free flow of global capital and the risk this might pose to their political autonomy. This post-war rebuilding did indeed see economies around the world return to vigorous growth for the first time since before the Great Depression. Over the decades of ensuing growth until the 1970s, Germany and Japan, for instance, caught up to the United States in terms of technological advances, first by exploiting economies of scale in production and second by utilising the comparative advantage of a highly educated workforce and residual manufacturing expertise. These led to a significant increase in GDP, and in areas like consumer electronics and automobiles this production led to an excess supply that required the development of new international markets to absorb it.

Interestingly, Williamson (2002) notes that *'From the very beginning in the 1940s the General Agreement on Tariffs and Trade explicitly excused low-income countries from the need to dismantle their import barriers and exchange controls. This GATT permission served to lower GDP in low-income countries below what might have been, but the permission was consistent with the anti-global ideology prevailing in previously-colonial Asia and Africa, in Latin America where the great depression hit so hard, and in Eastern Europe dominated as it was by the state-directed USSR. Thus, the succeeding rounds of liberalization over the first two decades or so of GATT brought freer trade and gains from trade mainly to OECD markets. However, these facts do not show that late twentieth century globalization favored rich countries. Rather, they show that globalization favored all (industrial) countries who liberalized and penalized those (pre-industrial) who did not.'*

During the 1970s the post-war global economy encountered an important crisis: the breakdown of the Bretton Woods system when the U.S. closed the gold window. As the dollar relinquished its role as the currency which all others were measured against and as the provider of global parity with gold, exchange rates were forced to float freely. With no need to modulate dollar convertibility into gold any longer, the U.S. removed its capital controls in 1974 and let dollars flow freely around the world. This led to many countries following suit, first Great Britain in 1979 and numerous other European countries during the mid-1980s. With gold no longer acting as a brake on money printing, however, high inflation ensued, which led to currency fluctuations and mass unemployment as companies struggled to survive. Ove Kaj Pedersen (Konkurrencestaten, 2010) argues that this period represented a transition from the post-war order to our present global order. Whereas the United States was the dominant global power after World War II, now, in an intriguing turn of events, the losers of the war, Germany and Japan, began to rise and the economic and monetary integration of Europe began to gather force.

It should be noted that the coordination among European currencies, which began in 1978, several years after the gold standard was abandoned, took place within the so-called *'snake'*. Also known as the European Exchange Rate Mechanism, or ERM, this was a forex trading band within which currencies could fluctuate. This coordination period therefore saw the gradual decline of national sovereignty over the European currencies, as well as a diminution of control over the increased capital flows which accompanied the financial market deregulation of the 1980s and 1990s.

Finally, it should be mentioned that the United States, despite its declining hegemony in regard to global trade, nonetheless maintained a very dominant position in global finance due to the attractiveness of its financial markets, the strength of its financial institutions, and size of the its economy.

1.5   Most Recent Era: The Second Wave of Globalisation

Beginning in the 1980s, the rapid industrialisation which had taken the West by storm a hundred years before exploded across the developing world. Driven by the low labour costs of a poor, abundant populace competing for good jobs, China, India, and Brazil dramatically increased their manufacturing base and skill level. As Western corporations perceived the cost savings opportunity presented by moving factories abroad, they closed operations in North America and Europe, leading to a moderate de-industrialisation on these continents. The winners were the Asian economies as the balance of trade tilted forcefully in their favour and their many workers who saw their standards of living increase. Meanwhile, their counterparts in the industrialised world lost ground as their political leaders inveighed against the outsourcing of manufacturing jobs but were unable to reverse the trend. Ultimately, this shift in the balance of global trade from West to East can be seen through Asia and the Middle East's increase on a trade-weighted basis over the period, with Asia showing particular strength in industrial goods and the Middle East in energy and metals. In the meantime, North America's relative share of trade has declined, while Europe has maintained its overall position.

Furthermore, it is interesting to note that trade volumes for countries within the Organisation for Economic Co-operation and Development (OECD) - which includes the world's wealthiest countries and in essence is shorthand for the West - saw a decline in trade from 2008 to 2015, whereas Asia and Latin America saw a significant increase.

Throughout the 1980s and 1990s, more and more emerging markets became integrated into the global economy, starting with the Asian Tigers of South Korea, Taiwan, Hong Kong, and Singapore, and continuing with the rest of Asia and Latin America. Of special note is China, which experienced a meteoric rise in per-capita GDP. Beginning from under USD 200 in 1980 it rose to over USD 8,000 in 2016 (World Bank), which is unprecedented in world history. As these economies grew, global trade increased and FDI accelerated, especially from the 1990s onwards as shown earlier. Not coincidentally, it was at the height of this activity, in 1994, that both the European Economic Area and the North America Free Trade Agreement (NAFTA) were adopted.

During this period of expanded international trade, some of the most important geopolitical events of the second half of the 20th century took place. The Berlin Wall came down in 1989, communism collapsed across Eastern Europe the following year, and the Soviet Union was dissolved in 1991. In the ensuing years these newly liberalised economies which previously comprised the Iron Curtain countries gave new impetus to the march of globalisation, and by 2012 Russia itself was accepted into the World Trade Organisation.

This period saw the rise of China, Germany and Japan as exporting nations, with the U.S. and United Kingdom reducing their relative positions.

Table 4. Top Trading Nations - Exports in USD (Billions)

1950		2007	
United States	47.8	China	1,429
United Kingdom	44.2	Germany	1,243
France	21.1	United States	1,199
South Africa	19.0	Japan	763
Canada	18.2	France	594
Germany	14.5	Italy	485
Australia	10.9	Netherlands	470
Netherlands	10.4	Canada	449
USSR/Russia	9.8	United Kingdom	410
Belgium	9.8	South Korea	383

Source: Maddison, Oxford Economics
Numbers in 2010 prices and exchange rate

Modern globalisation has done for today's Information Age what the pre-World War I integration of the global economy did for the Industrial Revolution: It has dispersed the benefits of technological change throughout the world and reinforced the importance of technology in improving standards of living. Moreover, this globalisation has contributed to a remarkable 40-year period of worldwide economic growth. As before, however, these benefits have been unevenly distributed in ways that often parallel the pre-WWI era. In general, poorer countries which have liberalised their economies and joined the group of freely trading nations have tended to grow more quickly than the more advanced economies, albeit from a much lower starting point. Generally speaking, newly emerging Asia and Eastern Europe are responsible for the lion's share of this normalisation with the historically industrialised world, but glaring gaps persist in average living standards between the emerging and advanced economies.

Looking within individual countries it is clear that income inequality has risen sharply over the past three to four decades. This is especially true in the developed world as upper-income people have reaped disproportionate gains, thereby causing the metrics of inequality to retreat to levels not seen since the early 20th century. Inequality trends within poorer, emerging economies has followed a mixed path, but inequality has widened the most quickly in countries like China where GDP has risen most sharply. Bucking the previous era's trend, however, are other nations, especially many in Latin America, which were not as poor as others to begin with and have seen their level of inequality narrow.

Regarding these phenomena, economist Richard Baldwin of the Graduate Institute of Economic Studies in Geneva argues (2006), that a concept called unbundling is behind the current wave of globalisation. In this paradigm, the different elements of production are divided into separate tasks and spread around the world, to whatever locale is most advantageous in terms of skill level and cost. Baldwin argues that unbundling began in the 1980s when a marked decline in transportation and communication costs exposed increased wage gaps between the industrialised and developing nations. These differentials made the offshoring of labour-intensive jobs more attractive to multinational corporations who could then earn higher profits. No longer was David Ricardo's classical theory of comparative advantage among the nations the main determinant of outsourcing. Rather, with the advance of information technology not just manufacturing but also administrative tasks could now be outsourced in the modern economy. In short, unbundling causes global competition to take place on a much more granular level because it is now **tasks**, and not just **sectors**, which compete for business around the globe. The impact of unbundling is that it is harder to predict the winners and losers of globalisation because offshoring is more sudden and less predictable. Inexpensive communication costs and management systems can tip the feasibility of transferring accounting tasks, R&D, or a specific manufacturing process to an overseas location. Baldwin further argues that given the finer resolution at task level 'inside the firm', global competition is now taking place between individuals at the task level instead of at the firm or sector level. From a historical perspective, trade models can be seen as shifting their focus from countries to industries to firms, and now to individuals.

In summary, today's globalised economy enables companies to conduct a vast array of activities without the limitations of geography. They can easily relocate various operations overseas, sell products, invest in equipment, search for employees, buy raw materials, and utilise technology with a reach and scale that was unimaginable only 30 years ago. This flexibility allows them to move business activities to wherever efficiencies are greatest, and many are doing this as they use the world's interconnectedness to develop supply chains which are global in their scope. In fact, with information and communication technology (ICT), the internet, and today's significantly lower transportation and communication costs, even smaller companies can export, produce offshore, or invest abroad. For instance, there is no cost penalty for sending an email from Copenhagen to Nairobi versus Århus; both are completely free. As a result, the exchange of ideas and innovation has risen exponentially since it has become essentially costless to access information and exchange ideas with anyone in the world.

1.6 Global Value Chains

This unbundling of activities involved in the manufacture of a product enables its associated tasks to be carried out entirely within a company or else sliced into elements which can be performed by other entities. When activities are divided between companies, we say that value chains are created. This division of production means that companies can buy semi-finished goods from elsewhere and use them in the manufacture of new products.

The way in which national economies have begun to specialise in increasingly specific tasks and product components is reflected in their global value chains and offshoring trends. To illustrate this point, in recent years Denmark has evolved into a significant sub-supplier for the German automobile industry. As a result, a large amount of Danish exports to Germany comprise highly specialised inputs into German industrial production which is subsequently exported from Germany to other countries. Thus, Denmark has become an indirect exporter to any country that purchases German cars.

Another example of a global value chain can be illustrated by the import of Ghanaian cocoa beans to a Danish chocolate manufacturer. After these beans have been processed into chocolate in Denmark, the chocolate is exported to Poland for final packaging, then sold to France for consumption. In other words, a product that begins as an import to Denmark has value added to it before export, sees further value added in a third country, and then is consumed in a fourth. This shows what is meant by indirect export and trade. A study by the Danish central bank, Danmarks Nationalbank (1st Quarter, 2016), reveals that the share of foreign value added to a given country's exports is greater for smaller economies. This is because the quantity of raw materials and semi-finished goods is lower for smaller economies, which means there is a greater need to purchase raw materials or semi-finished goods from other countries. The share of foreign value added to exports of the countries analysed in the study has risen between 1995 and 2011, which is an indication of this trend towards increased specialisation of tasks.

Recent years have seen companies developing much more sophisticated organisational approaches in their effort to serve global markets. Even smaller companies today do not operate merely domestically but rather through global value chains with an expanded network of suppliers, manufacturers, and distributors. A home goods company today may have its headquarters in Denmark, source most of its products from Asia, locate its finance department in Poland, produce its marketing material in Vietnam, have warehouse facilities in Denmark, Ukraine, and Portugal, and operate retail outlets worldwide.

This unbundling of the value chain and the advances of the Information Age have made it possible to outsource almost any task. From accounting to product design, engineering to financial analysis, or customer support to specialised manufacturing, the interconnectedness of today's world opens up new ways of doing business for companies large and small. As this takes place, it becomes more difficult to categorise products and services as being made in a certain country or performed in a specific location; rather, they are comprised of task elements which could be completed anywhere in world. This is true for automobiles, clothing, smart phone apps, and furniture. It also applies to business consulting, website design, and bookkeeping, just to name three services among a thousand. The list of possibilities is literally endless and becomes even more so each year.

Notwithstanding the increasing trend towards unbundling, in recent years there has been a focus on returning manufacturing from overseas to the West. One reason is that the wage gap has been narrowing between traditional outsource destinations like Mexico and China as wages have risen there but stagnated in the developed world. Distance, too, has played a role due to the time-in-transit required between production and delivery to destination markets. Time zone differences between widely disparate locations have been cited as a factor as well, since they demand expensive management time and technical resources in order to be overcome. Lastly, technological progress in robotics and automation has increasingly marginalised the impact of labour costs across a variety of industries and thus made it feasible to relocate manufacturing back to relatively high wage countries.

1.7 Globalisation and Economic Interdependence among Nations

The Great Recession of 2007, followed by the global financial crisis of 2008 provides a clear example of the interdependence among nations and economies. The sub-prime housing market collapse in the United States led to mortgage defaults there, which precipitated a recession and banking crisis. This crisis quickly spread to Europe since many of its banks had joined the real estate lending syndicates which made the failed U.S. loans. These losses in turn severely impacted the banks' balance sheets, which caused banking liquidity to dry up almost overnight. Meanwhile, when banks are not able to lend, corporations cannot continue to operate smoothly. This led to a panic in September 2008 which spread rapidly across the United States and Europe, and then the rest of the world. Even small, healthy economies like Iceland which had been expanding in previous years were impacted by the financial crisis and suffered a serious contraction.

During the Great Recession the U.S. Federal Reserve loosened its monetary policy by decreasing interest rates and pursuing so-called quantitative easing (QE). This expanded the supply of U.S. dollars as the Fed purchased bonds in order to promote increased investment and consumption in the nation's economy, which in turn was designed to jump-start economic growth. According to classical macroeconomic theory, an increase in the supply of dollars means that more of them must chase a fixed quantity of goods, which implies a depreciation in the value of the dollar on the forex markets. This would be positive for American exporters since they could then sell their products more easily abroad given that a weaker dollar means lower prices when translated to foreign currencies. On the other hand, a weaker dollar would have the opposite effect on goods exported to the United States by other countries – their goods would become more expensive in dollar terms and import volumes could be expected to shrink. Thus, it was that a macroeconomic policy decision in the United States, driven by domestic economic conditions and concerns, had a direct impact on the entire world in terms of exports, income, and employment.

While cross-border capital flows – especially FDI – can have a positive effect on economic growth, the volatility of these flows can undermine macroeconomic stability. This is especially true in developing countries since their economies are smaller and can thus be whipsawed more easily by the ebbs and flows of capital seeking a higher return. Macroeconomic stability can also be undermined by the exchange rate fluctuations which these cross-border capital movements cause. If movements are large relative to the size of an economy, depending on the capital flow's direction there will be significantly stronger or weaker demand for the local currency coming from abroad which will drive it up or down respectively. Consequently, periods of reduced cross-border capital inflows or net outflows are associated with currency depreciation, while greater inbound flows result in currency appreciation. Countries whose economies are highly dependent on foreign capital for GDP growth can therefore be severely impacted by a sudden halt or reversal in capital flows from abroad, as these changes can drive severe declines in exchange rates, asset prices, and real economic growth.

In addition, research conducted by the Bank of International Settlements (BIS) shows that the most volatile debt-related flows are largely pro-cyclical, which can exacerbate domestic economic cycles. Developing countries that lack the institutional and structural readiness to absorb capital inflows or outflows may be particularly vulnerable to these sudden shocks. However, the challenge is not only one of establishing the right institutions within a country; additionally, the institutions must ensure that their approach with regard to domestic financial systems is balanced on both a macroeconomic and microeconomic level (*The New Dynamics of Financial Globalisation*, 2017).

To illustrate these points, studying the U.S. Federal Reserve's actions in 2017 is instructive. The Fed began to increase interest rates that year for the first time since the 2008 global financial crisis and tapered its quantitative easing program to reduce its monetary expansion policy. It took these actions because it saw U.S. economic growth finally improving after years of sluggish performance, and in periods of growth, rates tend to gradually increase which then tightens the supply of money. This rise in interest rates and the corresponding reduced supply of money would be expected to increase the attractiveness of dollars and thus lead to their purchase on the forex markets; this in turn would cause the dollar to appreciate. This currency movement, however, does not take place in a vacuum. Rather, as the dollar rises against other currencies, these other currencies must fall. The result is that in South Africa, for example, billions of dollars that have been parked there for years may suddenly exit in pursuit of higher U.S. interest rates. This can create an overwhelming surge in the supply of South African Rand as investors sell Rand and lead to a swift depreciation– all without any policy changes whatsoever being made in South Africa. This shows the interdependence of macroeconomic policy in a globalised economy where capital flows freely, where monetary policy is independent and where currencies are traded without restriction. Also, we see once again that globalisation has winners and losers. In this example, U.S. exporters lose because their products become more expensive overseas, while foreign exporters to the U.S. win because their products are now cheaper for U.S. consumers to buy. However, if a given developing country's economy is heavily weighted towards dollar-denominated investments, its economy as a whole might lose if large amounts of capital suddenly exit as these dollars return to the U.S. from abroad.

1.8   Globalisation and Nation-States

In previous sections we discussed the effect of globalisation on economies and the production value chain, as well as the impacts on globalisation of political decisions and hegemonic power. In this section we analyse an underlying force behind these latter elements – that of the nation-state.

We begin with the concept of a **nation.** This is classically defined as comprised of the people inhabiting a certain geographical area who share common cultural traits such as language or descent. The **state,** meanwhile, refers to the political framework and governmental institutions which hold the reins of power and administer law within a specific area. Putting these two together, a **nation-state** is a sovereign entity with defined borders whose people share a common heritage and have formed a state governed by their leaders. The overlap between nation and state may be more or less strong for a given country, with the degree often depending on how much its people have in common and what type of government holds power.

From a historical perspective the nation-state is a relatively recent phenomenon which began in the Middle Ages and developed over time. During this epoch, there were numerous non-sovereign states in Europe where kings, emperors, noblemen, and the Church shared intertwining powers. Soon after the Renaissance period, from about 1650 to 1850, territorial states became widespread and acted as regional powers. Finally, in the second half of the 19th century these territorial states coalesced into what we know today as countries, with a majority of the population sharing a common history, language, religion, culture, and race. Denmark, for its part, is an example of an early regional power and nation-state, as Queen Margrethe I united Denmark, Norway, Sweden, Finland, the Faroe Islands, Iceland, and Greenland under the Danish crown in the 14th century. During the Protestant Reformation, Denmark was further unified as a nation in 1536 when it adopted Lutheranism as its common religion.

It is often said that the French Revolution at the close of the 18th century played a pivotal role in the development of the modern nation-state. The centuries-old notion that monarchs had a divine right to rule was overturned in a frenzy of violent catharsis. Democracy ultimately prevailed and the French populace, together with the newly born United States of America, declared that sovereign powers should emanate from the will and consent of the people. An identification with the nation-state had begun and the cultural make-up of a geographical area would have direct influence henceforth on how a nation-state was structured.

One hundred fifty years later, as Europe divested itself of its colonies in the aftermath of World War II, a wave of independence swept Africa and Asia which led to a dramatic rise in the number of nation-states. This phenomenon was repeated 40 years later when the Berlin Wall came down in 1989, followed by the collapse of the Soviet Union in 1991. This four-fold increase in the number of nation-states since the close of World War II to the present day's 193 members can be seen in the chart below.

The concept of globalisation can present a challenge to the nation-state for a number of reasons. For one, the flow of people across borders creates a less homogeneous so ciety which may weaken the existing national identity over time. Also, as people are exposed to globalisation the individual in a given nation-state may more easily identify with cultures or groups that transcend the nation, such as a global youth culture, global economists, global environmentalists, etc. Economists debate whether globalisation gradually reduces the individual's attachment to a national identity or whether national identity will prevail as the nation-state adapts to these new challenges. Regardless, most agree that the nation-state loses a degree of its autonomy under globalisation because of the increased interdependence between countries. One result is that politicians often have less direct influence on their constituents and may lose the ability to govern their people effectively. This can be especially true for smaller countries, which as noted previously, often experience a greater degree of globalisation than larger ones.

Figure 6. U.N. Member States

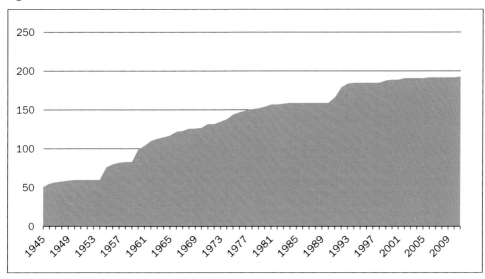

Source: United Nations

Katzenstein (1985) argues that, '*Exposed to global markets that they cannot control, the small European states have accommodated themselves to a situation that Americans are now beginning to experience as a crisis.*' Seen from this perspective, the European Union can be regarded as an entity which requires its nation-state to relinquish a certain degree of sovereignty in exchange for membership in a common, overarching institution where they have a voice and whose direction they may seek to influence.

Pedersen (Konkurrencestaten, 2010) argues that a new order for the global economy began to dawn in the two-year period from 1993 to 1995: in February 1993, newly elected U.S. President Bill Clinton introduced his economic program by talking about *'a global economy in which we must compete with nations around the world'*. Several months later, in June, the president of the newly established European Commission, Jacques Delors, sounded the starting gun for the 'competitive race' between Europe, the United States, and Japan as he called for Europe's single market to be fully implemented. This same month saw the development of the Copenhagen Criteria – a landmark agreement which defined the rules for EU membership and set the stage for the newly democratised Central and Eastern European countries (sans Russia) to join. New paradigms like the European Union were instituted and expanded, immediately after the old ones, especially Communism as symbolised by the Berlin Wall, Iron Curtain, and Soviet Union, had been swept away. Indeed, a new world order had begun.

Pedersen also talks about the 'competitive state' where politics are focused on optimising the global competitiveness of a nation's economies and corporations. In this arena, economics forms a central part of government policy. An illustration of this could be the Danish labour market system known as 'flexicurity'. Flexicurity combines welfare policies in the form of state-sponsored social security to the unemployed with flexible labour markets. One of the objectives is to optimise the global competitiveness of Danish companies and provide value-added training and education programmes which allow the efficient re-introduction of the unemployed into the labour force once again. Because globalisation leads to specialisation and consequently changes the need for labour in various sectors of an economy, some sectors will win while others lose. Consequently, it is therefore imperative that labour markets be flexible so that workers can transition in a timely manner and develop skills which will be rewarded in the economy going forward. Labour market policies can therefore be seen as part and parcel of a nation's competitive advantage.

FLEXICURITY

Flexicurity is sometimes described by saying, 'People have the right to education and social protection and a duty to work and contribute to society' (P.N. Rasmussen 2007, Danish Prime Minister 1993-2001). It is based on the following four pillars;

1) Reduced regulation of the labour market. (For example, Denmark does not have an officially mandated minimum wage)
2) Protection of employees through unemployment benefits and the welfare system
3) Active labour market programmes which match unemployed workers with available jobs
4) Attraction of new industries and promotion of education and job skills training

The challenges that globalisation can pose to a nation-state's competitiveness often lead to a situation where the state becomes directly involved in policies which affect its companies' positioning within the global markets. It can thus be argued that the scope of global competitiveness today has expanded to include a variety of institutional aspects for a given country. A good example is the annual *Global Competitiveness Report* produced by the World Economic Forum. This report ranks 137 countries on their level of national competitiveness as defined by the set of institutions, policies, and factors which determine their degree of productivity. A wide variety of rankings exist for other criteria as well – e.g., the World Bank's *'Ease of Doing Business Index'*; the OECD's *'Better Life Index'*; and the United Nations' *'Human Development Index'*, just to name a few. Consequently, we see that global economics and competitiveness play out today in a much more institutionalised setting than in the past because of the way in which economic and nation-state dynamics are intertwined.

1.9 Wealth and Global Income Distribution

International trade is vital to a nation's growth and prosperity. It increases specialisation according to comparative advantages, improves the allocation of resources, and can offer economies of scale. Specialisation and competition in turn often lead to increased innovation and new products, which result in a beneficial cycle of higher productivity and greater national income. Denmark, for example, offers an illustrative case study. In recent decades it has gradually begun to manufacture increasingly advanced products such as pharmaceuticals, wind turbines, and food enzymes. Given Denmark's small population of 5.8 million people, most of these products are naturally sold abroad as exports. At the same time, international trade has made the import of relatively less costly goods from China and India available to Danish consumers. This dynamic improves Denmark's terms of trade (defined as export prices relative to import prices), while simultaneously increasing the standard of living in each of these three countries as production is allocated to the country where it is comparatively most advantageous to manufacture it. It should be noted that as the production of less costly goods in Denmark moves to China and India, Danish jobs naturally exit with them. Consequently, employees and business owners in import-focused industries are prone to suffer from globalisation, whereas their counterparts in China and India will likely gain. Conversely, the sectors of the Danish economy dedicated to producing advanced products and exports will benefit as more business flows to them from around the world. The fact that Danish society has benefited from globalisation on balance is therefore likely linked to the relatively efficient means it has developed of assisting negatively impacted people through programs such as the flexicurity discussed in Section 1.8.

Because globalisation and international trade generate economic growth, most countries have experienced wealth creation and rising Gross Domestic Product (GDP) as a result. A nation's economic wealth is traditionally measured by its aggregate output in the form of GDP, which measures the total formal output of an economy. Notwithstanding, globalisation is also a disruptive force, and the specialisation it brings will lead to winners and losers as exemplified above. This in turn can increase the level of income inequality within nations, which may provoke resistance to globalisation within society. GDP is typically adjusted for differences between countries in the price of a basket of goods and services because buying these goods in Copenhagen will likely be more expensive than in, say, Ouagadougou. Adjusting for those differences is done by comparing 'Purchasing Power Parities', or PPP. GDP adjusted for PPP varies significantly between countries as illustrated in the table below and shows that the average income level per capita is nearly 28 times higher in Denmark than in Burkina Faso.

Understanding the factors that make a country wealthy is a complicated topic. Classical macroeconomics typically uses the Solow model to describe how poorer countries can theoretically catch-up to wealthier ones if they pursue identical policies in regards to savings and capital accumulation. So, if savings rates are low or capital markets are inefficient then the rate of investment will also be low, which hinders capital accumulation through productive investments. Ultimately, deploying capital productively is one way in which nations can become wealthier and close an income gap with their peers.

Table 5. GDP per capita (PPP, current international USD)

Country	1990	2016
Burkina Faso	546	1,771
Canada	20,108	44,820
China	987	15,529
Côte d'Ivoire	2,064	3,693
Denmark	18,225	49,029
India	1,134	6,571
Peru	3,434	13,019
Portugal	11,769	30,659
Russian Federation	8,013	24,789
Thailand	4,298	16,913
Turkey	6,146	25,247
United States	23,955	57,638

Source: The World Bank Database

Global trade is another path to wealth, particularly for smaller countries who embrace globalisation and pursue specialised production, economies of scale, and productivity growth. Other countries may be blessed with abundant natural resources such as oil and gas, ore deposits, arable land, and labour. In these cases, internal factors such as high labour force participation, strong manufacturing productivity, and adherence to the rule of law will elevate one country over another in terms of relative economic development and wealth.

Apart from optimising land, labour, and capital as the classical factors of production, a country's total economic output – known as total factor productivity, or TFP – will vary from country to country for exogeneous reasons related to the political and institutional structures in a given nation. These will be our focus in the following section.

1.10 Political and Economic Institutions

In their acclaimed book, *Why Nations Fail (2012)*, economist Daron Acemoglu from MIT and political scientist James Robinson from the University of Chicago argue that, '*Nations fail economically because of extractive institutions. These institutions keep countries poor and prevent them from embarking on a path to economic growth.*' Although specific conditions differ, according to the authors this explains why many nations in Africa and South America fare relatively badly, as can be seen in the cases of Venezuela, Zimbabwe, and Egypt. Acemoglu & Robinson refer to the 'iron law of oligarchy', whereby political elites concentrate resources at the top and monopolise power. Using their wealth and influence in concert with corruption, they extract economic rent for themselves and for their cronies. This impoverishes the country over time because there is no incentive for individuals to take the risk of building a business or to foster the type of creative destruction which an economy needs to grow. According to Acemoglu et al., although extractive economic institutions can generate short-term growth as national economies are built up by centrally controlled political institutions, they will fail in the long run due to this lack of creative destruction.

In his research, Mogens Justesen of Copenhagen Business School (2010) argues that,

'The basic importance of the state consists in the fact that the state has a (legitimate) monopoly on the use of coercion within a designated geographical area. This provides the state apparatus and its organizations – courts, bureaucratic agencies and police – with unique authority and power to handle conflicts between citizens and solve collective action problems. A strong state with strong capacities is therefore a necessary condition for property rights to be credibly enforced. However, a strong state is also a potential threat to property rights. The problem is that a state that is strong enough to protect and enforce property rights is also strong enough to transgress against those very rights and appropriate the wealth and investments of citizens. This creates a fundamental political dilemma, since the presence of a strong state is necessary for both the enforcement and protection of property rights, but at the same time the powers and coercive capabilities vested in the state can also be used to undermine the institutional foundation of economic development.'

Justesen continues by saying,

'The state and government must also commit to enforcing and protecting property rights in the future. This problem concerns the so-called time inconsistency problem. In essence, it concerns how citizens and investors can be sure that the state will also enforce and protect the set of status quo property rights in the future, and not use its unique coercive capabilities to expropriate wealth and investments. This problem is highly relevant since many investments possess a dynamic element, meaning that potential payoffs from current activities can only be reaped in the future. Thus, if citizens and investors anticipate that the government does not have an incentive to protect property rights in the future, the result may be decreasing investment levels'

Justesen, 2010

In addition to respect for the rule of law and strong property rights, another institutional framework required for economic growth is judicial independence. A state whose judiciary can be co-opted by its rulers or suborned in exchange for money or influence will not render impartial judgments or give confidence to investors. Lastly, the final institutional pillar which robust economies around the world share is a regulatory structure and bureaucratic system which provide society with fair, efficient controls and proper enforcement of laws so that commerce can be conducted without favouritism, bribery, or excessive procedural delays.

Apart from the institutions themselves, efficient economies depend on intermediaries like labour unions, credit ratings, third-party certifications, transaction facilitators, auditors, banks, etc. to provide the structures for a well-functioning economy. These intermediaries are sometimes missing or weak, making it possible for informal institutions to emerge instead. This creates so-called institutional voids, where an unfair playing field is accessible only to a select group of local actors. Institutional voids invariably lead to increased transaction costs for doing business in a country and can hinder the rationality of market participants since it is difficult to act rationally in an unpredictable environment. Not only is this time-consuming and a drain on limited resources, but it also tends to foster a high incidence of corruption.

A classic example of the way institutions can develop along very disparate paths with far-reaching implications for the future can found in comparing Latin America to the United States. Both were colonised in the 16th or early 17th century by European powers. Both gained independence within the past 200 to 250 years. Lastly, both enjoy a great abundance of natural resources and have large populations. However, the United States is far wealthier and has lower income inequality than Latin America precisely because the political and economic institutions it established centuries ago were not founded on an extractive footing but rather on one that shared power within a stable, three-pronged system with appropriate checks and balances on the executive, judicial, and legislative branches. Thanks to this foundation, the United States gradually became the wealthiest nation in the history of the world, while Latin America continues to struggle with high levels of corruption and subpar economic performance.

Moving from past generations to the present, Acemoglu & Robinson (2012) write:

'The economic institutions in the United States enabled those men to start companies with ease, without facing insurmountable barriers. Those institutions also made the financing of their projects feasible. The U.S. labor markets enabled them to hire qualified personnel, and the relatively competitive market environment enabled them to expand their companies and market their products. These entrepreneurs were confident from the beginning that their dream projects could be implemented: they trusted the institutions and the rule of law that these generated and they did not worry about the security of their property rights. Finally, the political institutions ensured stability and continuity. For one thing, they made sure that there were no risk of a dictator taking power and changing the rules of the game, expropriating their wealth, imprisoning them or threatening their lives and livelihoods. They also made sure that no particular interest in society could warp the government in an economically disastrous direction, because political power was both limited and distributed sufficiently broadly that a set of economic institutions that created the incentives for prosperity could emerge.'

Why Nations Fail, 2012: 76

We now turn our attention to Egypt. Egypt lies at the crossroads of the Middle East and Africa and was home in ancient times to the world's first imperial power. However, like Latin America, Egypt today offers a compelling counterpoint to the United States because of its weak institutional frameworks. The mere incorporation of a company can take considerable time due to delays from bureaucratic red-tape, which serves as a breeding ground for corruption. The company might be unable to finance its investment project domestically and require foreign financing, with the attendant currency risks of earning revenues in Egyptian pounds but repaying loans in dollars or euros. Meanwhile, the market the company wishes to enter will probably be dominated by state-owned enterprises (SOEs), with even the military involved in economic production, thereby creating an opaque market environment with no clear-cut competitive landscape. Moreover, the rule of law will be discovered to be weak, with property rights not guaranteed and investor protections uncertain. A very real example could involve a new city road – unplanned at the project's commencement – whose construction path cuts directly through the project worksite, thereby obliging project investors to move to a new location at their own expense. Finally, political instability will pose a substantial risk and may result in one of the project's promoters being imprisoned in connection with a court case following the so-called Arab Spring revolution of 2011. All of these things have actually happened and they can drive investors away, with deleterious consequences for Egypt's economy and the country as a whole.

Combining the lessons from these examples, we see that the differences between countries in the type and quality of their institutions create vastly different incentives for people to pursue an education, save, invest, innovate, start businesses, and take risks. All of these factors, taken together, have a profound impact on the country's economic growth and overall degree of prosperity.

Harvard economist Dani Rodrik (2003) notes that institutional structures and policies are not necessarily uniform across countries but in fact can vary by location. He supports this with the following statement, where he says, '*The experience of former socialist economies, discussed by George de Menil, further reinforces the role of local context. The three countries closest to Western Europe (Poland, Hungary, and Czech Republic) have done very well. What seems to have been key for these countries, as de Menil emphasizes, is their relationship with the European Union (EU). The EU provided a plausible institutional model for these countries, in view of a common historical heritage and relatively short experiences under Communism. Furthermore, this model was backed up with the carrot of eventual accession to the EU. Consequently, structural reform was effective and took hold relatively quickly in Poland, Hungary and Czech Republic.*'

Another example of this phenomenon could be Estonia, which has done very well since independence in 1991 compared to other post-Soviet countries such as Albania and Moldova.

SOVIET UNION TO RUSSIA

After the break-up of the Soviet Union the new Russian Federation sought to pursue market-oriented policies geared towards globalisation and economic reforms in order to integrate with the rest of the world economy. However, Russia's economy is heavily dependent upon commodities and resources - especially oil and natural gas. In addition, it is beset by a high concentration of economic and political power among relatively few actors who extract economic rent through the control of these assets, inasmuch as the incentive to drive economic reform by securing property rights, ensuring the rule of law, enforcing contracts, and promoting competition was low for those in power. Consequently, it can be argued that substantive reforms were never truly pursued in Russia and that the institutional structure has remained extractive, with a significant nexus between business, economics, and politics. This period can be characterised as the de-industrialisation of the Soviet Union, and it is estimated that today about 70% or more of economic output in Russia is controlled by state owned enterprises (SOEs). According to Freedom House (2017), Russia has experienced approximately ten years of reduced political, civil, and economic freedom.

According to Rodrik;

'Modest changes in institutional arrangements and in official attitudes towards the economy can produce huge growth payoffs. Deep and extensive institutional reform is not a prerequisite for a takeoff in growth. That is the good news. The bad news is that the required changes can be highly specific to the context. And for a good reason: the binding constraints on growth differs. The mark of a successful reform is its ability to concentrate effort on the binding constraints.'

He continues by adding,

'The process of escaping from low-level poverty traps may be fundamentally different from middle-income countries. The policies required to initiate a transition from a low-income equilibrium to a state of rapid growth may be qualitatively different from those required to reignite growth of a middle-income country. At low levels of income, with reasonable institutions and reasonable policies, it may be easy to achieve high growth up to semi-industrialization. But the institutional requirements of reigniting growth in a middle-income country can be significantly more demanding.'

Rodrik, 2003

Economic development may also go in the other direction as in the case of the collapse of Venezuela. As Ricardo Hausmann (in Rodrik, 2003) explains, starting in the 1950s Venezuela was seen as the most stable democracy in Latin America, with a strong political party system, free press, and solid labour and business institutions to negotiate social conflicts. Yet Venezuela, which once had the highest economic growth rates in Latin America, is now immeshed in a severe economic depression. What happened? Hausmann focuses on two explanations, both related to the fact that Venezuela saw sweeping radical shifts in politics when Hugo Chavez was elected president in 1999. The classic explanation is that a decline in oil exports reduced the revenues from this tremendously important revenue stream, and consequently led to a plunge in GDP. But Hausmann's calculations suggest that this cannot account for more than half of Venezuela's overall decline. The second factor, as he argues convincingly, is a rise in country risk. This is reflected in Venezuela's country rating and the interest rates demanded on the international market for hard currency loans, which have subsequently reduced the nation's capital stock. What lies behind this, according to Hausmann, is the inability to settle income distribution conflicts in a country where the populace became dependent upon government handouts when oil prices revenues were high, but which is now forced to fend for itself amid an endemically corrupt and increasingly dysfunctional society. Venezuela has simply become a riskier environment, which in turn has eroded the quality and legitimacy of public institutions to the point that the country is now on the brink of collapse.

In summary, globalisation creates opportunities and challenges, as well as winners and losers. Although it tends to increase the level of interdependence between countries, sometimes at a cost to national sovereignty, it also increases a nation's wealth provided that its political and institutional frameworks are well founded and the rule of law prevails. Ultimately these are the underpinnings which determine the progress of nations and the way in which the current wave of globalisation will impact the course of history.

CHAPTER 2

Trade Theory

By Mikkel Godt Gregersen, Ph.D., MBA, M.Sc.

Across the sweep of history people have engaged in trade for one primary reason: it increases wealth and utility. This, in turn, is made possible by the fact that each trading partner can provide goods and services that are different from one another. Whether conducted by countries, industries, companies, or individuals, trade is possible because the party on either side holds something of value to the other. Therefore, from a macro perspective, international trade increases a country's welfare because of the better allocation of resources it enables.

This chapter is dedicated to discussing some of the most important trade theories in Economics. Though the first of these originated in the 15th century, each of them nonetheless has relevance in our globalised world today. In this chapter we first study Mercantilism, Absolute and Comparative Advantages, and the Heckscher-Ohlin Theorem. From there we progress to the Standard Trade Model, Economies of Scale, Michael Porter's Diamond Model, and Product Spaces. We begin by briefly summarising the models and theories, then proceed to a more elaborate description of each.

Mercantilism is not so much a theory as a philosophy. Its premise is that nations should maximise wealth by accumulating gold and silver via trading profits. It prevailed throughout Europe for most of the colonial period, from the 1400s to the end of the 1700s. The idea was to promote exports from the New World colonies to Europe, while limiting imports through tariffs, in conjunction with legal and technical trade barriers.

Many people point to Adam Smith's seminal treatise, *The Wealth of Nations*, (1776) as marking the turning point away from Mercantilism towards a more market-based theory of economics and trade. We refer to this today as classical economics. As we shall see, Smith was an advocate of specialisation and argued that nations should produce in accordance with their *absolute advantages*.

Adam Smith is widely regarded as the father of classical economics. Looking at the world of his day, however, he did not realise that in the future some nations might be superior to others in all respects, which would leave no room for trade with less powerful countries who lacked absolute advantages. David Ricardo perceived this in 1819 and noted that nations should produce in accordance with their *comparative advantages*, which do not necessarily overlap with absolute advantages.

Both Smith's and Ricardo's theories were based on a framework consisting of one factor (labour), two countries, and two goods. In 1977 Swedish economist Bertil Ohlin (together with James E. Meade) received the Nobel Prize in Economics for developing what became known as the **Heckscher-Ohlin (H-O) Theorem**. The prize was awarded based on Ohlin's 1933 book explaining the theorem, which in turn was based on Heckscher's earlier work from 1919. The H-O Theorem builds on the Ricardian model and shows how nations trade not only in accordance with their comparative labour efficiency advantages, but also in accordance with their initial resource endowments, such as natural resources and population. The simplest form is a 2x2x2 model – two countries, two goods, two factors of production. The H-O model was later expanded by various economists, with the **Standard Trade Model** being one of the more prevalent adaptations – or it could be argued – one of the major generalisations.

In addition to the theoretical economic models just described, there are three other well-known frameworks for describing international trade which have gained currency in today's economic circles. They are empirical in nature, not theoretical, being based on observable situations and applicable across a wide array of contexts.

The first of these frameworks is known as **Economies of Scale.** These are said to exist when unit costs decrease as a function of greater volumes, and they can apply both to a single firm or to an entire industry. If a firm can operate at a cost advantage because of its size, it possesses internal economies of scale. If the whole industry, however, can operate a cost advantage it is referred to as an external economy of scale. The resulting cost advantages are useful in explaining why countries, particularly advanced ones, produce and trade some goods rather than others.

The second empirical framework was developed by Harvard economist Michael Porter and described in a 1990 article he wrote for the Harvard Business Review entitled, *The Competitive Advantage of Nations*. Known as the Diamond Model, it describes four factors which determine a nation's competitive advantage: **factor conditions, demand conditions, related or supporting industries, and firm strategy, structure, and rivalry**. In later years the model was extended to include **government** and **chance** as additional determining factors. In many ways Porter draws on all of the economic models mentioned previously, except for the Mercantilist approach.

One of the latest contributions to the discussion of economic trade theory is the *Product Space Framework*, published in 2007. This is not a theory per se, but rather an empirical analysis of a country's trading patterns. Its main assumption is that countries are more likely to begin producing goods which are closely related to those they already produce, rather than unrelated goods. This *proximity of goods* premise has proven to be a good predictor of a given country's growth, or lack thereof, over time.

2.1   Mercantilism

With the dawn of the 1400s came the Age of Discovery as Europe exited the Middle Ages and pushed beyond the boundaries of the then-known world. Armed with the astronomical compass, better ship designs, and improved map-making ability, Portuguese and Spanish sailors plied the oceans of the world in search of new frontiers from which to expand their royal sponsors' empires. As they explored the coasts of Africa and India, then the Americas, and finally circumnavigated the globe, their exploits captured the imagination of a European continent which, thanks to the newly invented printing press, could read their stories by the thousands. Soon the British, French, and Dutch followed suit and the race for imperial outposts and their wealth was on across the globe.

Needless to say, this colonisation of Africa, Asia, and the Americas permanently changed the world. Voluntarily or not, it led to the migration of millions of people and the creation of powerful new societies. Gold and silver were mined in quantities previously unimaginable and spices and silk became the luxuries of the day in European palaces.

The so-called Columbian Exchange also found its genesis in this colonial period. From the Americas came agricultural goods such as tobacco, pineapples, and cocoa. These were sent to Europe in exchange for manufactured goods and cattle, which arrived to the colonies as the foundation for further wealth creation on the backs of slaves or indigenous labour. In addition to slavery, one of the most unfortunate consequences of this global commerce was the spread of diseases like smallpox and typhus which decimated entire people groups of native Indians throughout North America, the Spanish colonies, and Brazil in a human cost whose toll will never fully be known.

The establishment of colonies throughout the world greatly increased global trade and prompted a wave of new commerce and trading practices in Europe during the 16th and 17th centuries. Many of these practices, which dramatically changed the economic landscape of Europe, still underpin the financial systems and market principles of today. Among these landmark changes was the ascent of **capitalism**. Capitalism is defined as an economic and political system where a country's trade and industry are controlled by private owners rather than the state. These owners are the individuals who take the initiative to begin new ventures and assume risks through investments intended to create wealth. Over the approximately 350 years it continued, colonialism, yoked to capitalism, created massive wealth for untold numbers of private merchants. These individuals took their profits, invested again, and constructed a system of commerce which changed the face of Europe and the world.

A second important development in business practices which transpired during this period was known as the **joint-stock company**. The joint-stock company was essentially the predecessor of the modern limited liability corporation, where people use the stock market to buy ownership shares and 'join' their wealth for a common investment opportunity. In Europe this common purpose was the colonisation of the globe. For instance, Jamestown, Great Britain's first colony in North America, was established through a joint-stock company in the early 1600s, as was its crown jewel, India, some 150 years later. The impact of a pool of investors joining their wealth is that it served to diversify risk across a range of expeditions, since both risk and expected returns were extremely high.

It was during this period that the nations of Europe adopted a new economic and trade policy known as **Mercantilism**. Mercantilism is the philosophy that a country's power depends mainly on its economic wealth. Wealth, which enables nations to build strong navies and purchase vital trade goods, in turn helps them gain power vis-à-vis other countries. According to Mercantilism, a nation can increase its wealth (and thus power) in two ways. Firstly, it can acquire as much gold and silver as possible. Secondly, it can establish a **favourable balance of trade** which it uses to accumulate bullion. Mercantilism implied that a nation's ultimate goal was to become self-sufficient, rather than reliant upon other countries for traded goods.

Naturally, Mercantilism and colonialism went hand in hand. Besides providing plenty of gold and silver, other raw materials like timber and animal pelts, which were in scarce supply back home, could be acquired in seemingly limitless quantities in the colonies. As time went by the colonies functioned both as a supplier of raw materials and a market for finished goods. The mother country would buy (or expropriate) the colonies' raw materials, then sell processed goods back to them at attractive margins which they enforced through trading policies. Mercantilism is therefore a very distinct type of **protectionism** which often involves the use of tariffs and restrictive trading rules. The economic revolution of Mercantilism spurred the growth of towns throughout Europe as a class of merchants who controlled great wealth brought commerce to the areas where they lived. However, although merchants, traders, and their suppliers enjoyed greatly improved living conditions, the majority of citizens remained mired in subsistence-level poverty. It would take a different system of economics for improved standards of living to trickle down to the masses.

In modern times, two large countries in particular, China and Germany, have been accused of applying mercantilistic principles. China, for instance, has been accused of surreptitiously accumulating a large stockpile of gold along with nearly $1.2 Trillion in U.S. Treasuries which some fear it may one day deploy as a currency weapon against the heavily debt-laden West. Both countries, meanwhile, have been criticised for running outsized trade surpluses with the rest of the world and not doing enough to open their borders for imports. They are targets mainly because they are the world's second and fourth largest economies, respectively, and run enormous trade surpluses year after year. Analysing more deeply though, these nations do not seem to be applying mercantilism but rather utilising untapped resources. China, for instance, has cheap, abundant labour due to its 1.3 billion population, many of whom are poor but very productive in their jobs. Consequently, it is a net saver nation which produces more than it consumes, and as such naturally generates large trade surpluses year after year.

Germany, for its part, faced great economic difficulty after its Reunification in 1990 as it sought to integrate an impoverished East Germany with highly developed

Figure 1. Trade Balances for Selected Countries

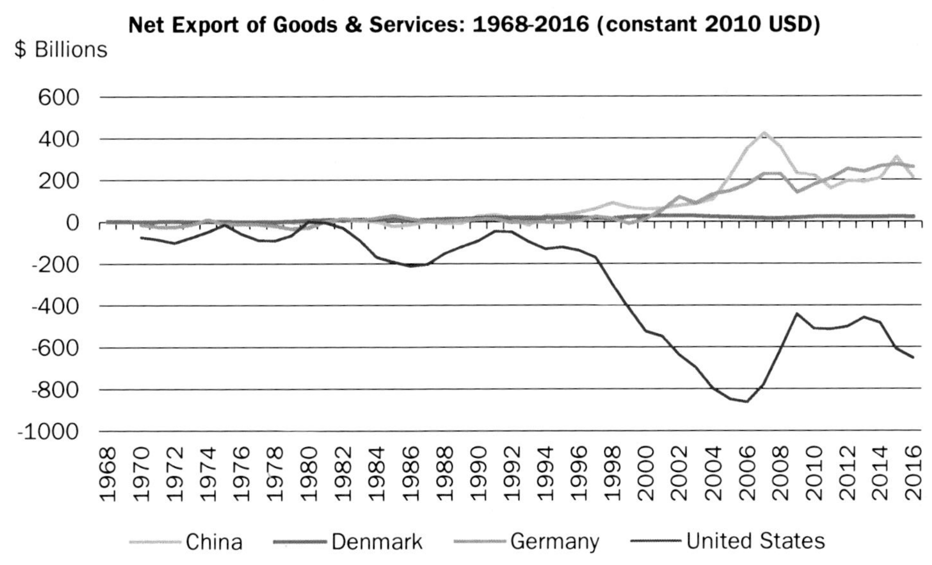

Net Export of Goods & Services: 1968-2016 (constant 2010 USD)

Source: The World Bank Data Bank

West Germany. The result was plunging labour productivity and soaring trade deficits as the reunification process continued. Two main factors have since put Germany back on track. The first was the introduction of the Euro in 1999 which opened the Eurozone to free trade and enabled export-led growth to lift the German economy. The second was the so-called Hartz labour reforms implemented in 2003 which combined unemployment benefits with pressure to work which in time turned the labour situation around.

Figure 1 shows trade balances for China, Germany, the United States, and Denmark in constant 2010 dollars from 1968 to today. It is easy to see why some economists and politicians feel that China's trade surpluses are too high. In percentage terms, though, Denmark is also running substantial trade surpluses (6% of GDP in 2016), yet because of its small economy it attracts little to no attention.

2.2 Adam Smith and Absolute Advantages

In his 1776 masterpiece, *The Wealth of Nations*, Adam Smith opposes Mercantilism as a viable economic theory. In his book, which is still regarded as the cornerstone of classical economic theory, Smith argues that international trade need not be a negative-sum game, or at best a zero-sum game. On the contrary it can be a positive-sum game where everyone wins if countries specialise in order to acquire **absolute advantages.**

Smith's treatise was written towards the beginning of the Industrial Revolution. In his reflections on economic affairs as this era began, Smith offered incisive perspectives on a broad array of topics such as the division of labour, productivity, and free markets. After developing these themes, he synthesised them into a trade theory where he introduced the concept that made him famous, known as the **division of labour**. Smith argued that specialisation via division of labour could dramatically increase the productivity of workers. Using the example of a pin factory he showed how labour productivity could increase by up to 4,800 times if the manufacture of pins was divided into 18 individual steps. Another well-known concept he introduced is that of the Invisible Hand – the idea that free markets will clear themselves by market mechanisms if permitted to do so, almost as though an **invisible hand** were guiding the market's price action as well as individuals' behaviour.

Smith's thoughts on the division of labour constitute the basis for his theory of international trade.[1] According to Smith, international trade is advantageous for nations because:

'[It] gives a value to their superfluities, by exchanging them for something else, which may satisfy a part of their wants, and increase their enjoyments. By means of it the narrowness of the home market does not hinder the division of labour in any particular branch of art or manufacture from being carried to the highest perfection. By opening a more extensive market for whatever part of the produce of their labour may exceed the home consumption, it encourages them to improve its productive powers, and to augment its annual produce to the utmost, and thereby to increase the real revenue and wealth of the society.'

WN, IV.i.31

Here, Smith connects international trade to his ideas about the division of labour. If trade with another nation is established, an extension of the division of labour will result since the international market is larger than the domestic market alone. International trade is therefore advantageous to a nation, Smith argues, because the division of labour between nations leads to an increase *'of the exchangeable value of the annual produce of the land and labour of the country'* (WN, IV.iii.c.3). In other words, the wealth of the nation and its people increases. Smith also mentioned an additional benefit of international trade, namely that it incentivises the transfer of technology and know-how between nations. This adoption and use of new production techniques leads to productivity growth and, consequently, to economic development and increased wealth. Smith pointed out that these advances in productivity and specialisation can be even more important to a nation than access to a wider market, especially for a large economy.

To summarise this section, Adam Smith's theory of international trade is dynamic in that it integrates well with the broader economic framework of the division of labour and considers the economic growth which results from, and affects, international trade. Furthermore, absolute production cost advantages and the division of benefits from trade are not permanently fixed but rather develop and emerge as a natural result of trade. The key to gaining absolute advantages is increased labour productivity, which in turn is acquired through investments in technology.

In analysing Adam Smith's impact on modern economics, it seems that most economics textbooks fail to capture this dynamic depth of Smith's theory of international trade. They tend to present it as essentially standardised and static, stating, for example, that the theory of absolute advantage *'can explain only a small part of world*

---

1. This argument follows Schumacher (2012).

trade' (Salvatore 2011, p.37). As a result, Smith's absolute advantage is seen as a special case of the theory of comparative advantage developed some 40 years later by Ricardo (as we shall see), and both theories are seen as complementary to one another (Dieckheuer 2001, p.50). Smith is often criticised for not having developed the more sophisticated theory of comparative advantage (Zhang 2008, p.3) and, in comparison to Ricardo, is described as a 'poor trade theorist' whose writings are dismissed as 'naive' (Mehmet 1999, p.47). However, these textbook accounts unfairly represent Smith's premise. In particular, they claim that trade is beneficial only because it leads to an increase in the number of commodities which can be produced with existing production technology and capabilities. This falls short of Smith's theory; it is not merely a simplification of it, but an erroneous interpretation. These textbooks only present a comparison of two static situations, i.e. before and after the opening of trade. Smith himself does not use this comparison or give a numerical example which reflects it. Moreover, the benefits a country receives in the form of technological change and economic growth are excluded altogether. Thus, the modern presentation lacks the depth and dynamic nature of Smith's original theory.

We now turn our attention in 'traditional' textbook fashion to Ricardo and the theory of **comparative advantages.**

2.3   Ricardo and Comparative Advantages

The concept of comparative advantages is at the same time refreshingly simple and utterly complex. This is probably why so many people seem to misunderstand it, even trained economists. In the words of economist and Nobel laureate Paul Krugman:

'Comparative advantage is a harder concept than it seems, because like any scientific concept it is actually part of a dense web of linked ideas. A trained economist looks at the simple Ricardian model and sees a story that can be told in a few minutes; but in fact, to tell that story so quickly one must presume that one's audience understands a number of other stories involving how competitive markets work, what determines wages, how the balance of payments adds up, and so on.'

MIT, Krugman, Ricardo

For our purposes, we presume that the audience has an understanding of economics and now proceed to explain the story of comparative advantages. We hasten to add, however, that the simple story is not by any means the whole story.

Imagine a world where there are only two countries, two goods, and one factor of production, called labour – in other words, the same setup which Adam Smith described. For our model we assume that each country produces computers and cloth.

The labour in Country A takes one hour to produce a computer and one hour to produce a unit of cloth. Country B, meanwhile, requires eight hours to produce a computer and two hours to produce one unit of cloth. This is summarised in the table below. Note that these numbers do not represent productivity, but rather its inverse – i.e., the number of hours required to produce a unit of output. In fact, productivity of labour depends on a country's technology level, which is why investments and access to technology are key determining factors in Ricardo's model.

Table 1. Labour Intensity in Production and Consumption Possibilities

	Computers	Cloth	Production Ratio = Relative Prices: P_{Comp}/P_{Cloth}	Assume 400 hours of labour available in each country	
				Maximum Computers	Maximum Units of Cloth
Country A	1 hr.	1 hr.	1	**400**	400
Country B	8 hrs.	2 hrs.	4	50	**200**

From this description it is clear that Country A has absolute advantages in producing both computers and cloth and would therefore. According to the static perception of Smith's theory of absolute advantages it would therefore have no interest in trading with Country B. However, let us assume that each country has 400 hours of labour available and that the demand for computers and cloth come in a complementary ra-

Figure 2. Production Possibility Frontiers for Two Different Countries

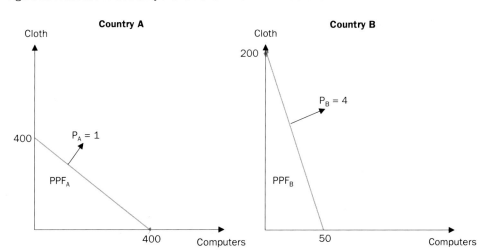

tio, which is to say that each country produces and consumes computers and cloth in a 1:1 ratio. In this case Country A would produce 200 of each good and Country B would produce 40 of each. This is straightforward to calculate because Country A needs two hours to produce a bundle of each, whereas Country B needs 10 hours to produce an identical bundle. The relative price in Country A for a unit of cloth to a computer would be $P_A = 1$, while the relative price in Country B would be $P_B = 4$. Note that this ratio is exactly the inverse of labour productivity. In Country A labour is equally productive in both computers and cloth, but in Country B the labour for cloth is four times more productive. This difference in relative labour productivity between the two countries is the reason they engage in trade; their difference in absolute labour productivity is not a consideration. The two countries' Production Possibility Frontiers (PPF) and their relative price of computers to cloth are shown in Figure 2 below.

Now assume that Countries A and B engage in trade.[2] For this to happen both nations need to benefit, or there would be no incentive for them to make the effort required. Fortunately, with their difference in comparative labour productivity, both countries *do* in fact have sufficient incentive. As Country A trades its cloth for the computers needed in Country B, it can get more cloth-per-computer in exchange (more than 1:1) than it could by producing cloth internally. For its part, as Country B trades it will receive more computers per unit of cloth (more than 1:4) than it could if its borders were closed.

In terms of trade negotiations, if Country A has all the bargaining power it can trade four units of cloth for one computer. On the other hand, if Country B has a much stronger hand it can trade one computer for one unit of cloth. These scenarios are outlined in Table 2. If the countries end up somewhere between these two 'Single Power Scenarios', the world equilibrium price will be established between 1 and 4, for example at $P_W = 2$. This is labelled as the 'Negotiated Power Scenario' which is outlined in Table 3 and Figure 3.

2. In order to analyze the effects of trade in the most realistic way possible, we need to assume that there are multiple Country B types. This is necessary so that Country A can trade as much as it wants to without being constrained by capacity limits in another country. This is not an unrealistic assumption by any means given that there are 195 countries in the world and 159 WTO members.

Table 2. Consumption Possibilities

Single Power Scenario	Country	Maximum # Computers	Maximum # Units of Cloth
Country A has all bargaining power	A	**400**	1600
	B	50	**200**
Country B has all bargaining power	A	**400**	400
	B	200	**200**

Table 3. Consumption Possibilities ($P_W = 2$)

Negotiated Power Scenario	Maximum # Computers	Maximum # Units of Cloth
Country A	**400**	800
Country B	100	**200**

The Production Possibility Frontier (PPF) and the Budget Constraint for the post-trade scenario is seen in Figure 3 below. If the areas under the PPF and Budget Constraint represent consumption possibilities before and after trade, respectively, in this stylised example each country will double its possible consumption. In other words, because of comparative advantage each country will dramatically increase its welfare by engaging in trade rather than closing its borders.

Figure 3. PPF, Budget Constraints, and Prices as a Function of Trade

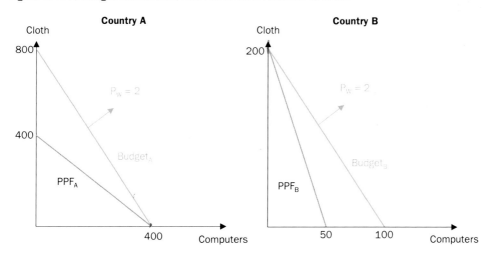

The economic reasoning behind comparative advantages is concerned with *opportunity costs*. Because labour is limited due to the assumption of perfect competition, when Country A produces one computer it loses the opportunity to produce a unit

of cloth (becausee of its 1:1 ratio production ratio). Country B, on the other hand, gives up four units of cloth for every computer produced due to its 4:1 ratio. As noted earlier these prices are relative, but they also reflect the opportunity cost of producing computers, as measured in lost production of cloth (and vice versa). Production of cloth is *comparatively* more expensive to produce in Country A because if it opts to produce computers instead it can trade these to Country B for *more* cloth than it could have produced on its own. On the other hand, computers are *comparatively* more expensive to produce in Country B for the same reason: it can obtain more computers by trading cloth to Country A than it could produce on its own.

In this simplified example, the world market price will find its equilibrium between one and four depending on respective bargaining power of Countries A and B. In more sophisticated Ricardian setups with more goods, the world market prices will be determined by the marginal labour productivity of the last traded good.

In the example outlined in Table 3 and Figure 3, both countries will produce in accordance with their respective comparative advantages. Consequently, Country A will only produce computers (400 units) and Country B will only produce cloth (200 units). As they trade they will do so at the relative price of one computer for two units of cloth. Assuming each country optimises its utility function by consuming bundles of equal amounts of computers and cloth, Country A can now consume 267 bundles (800/3), while Country B consumes 67 bundles (200/3). Country A gets 67 units more of each product, or 33% more than it could before trading began. Country B, in turn, will receive 27 more units of each, or 67% more compared to what it would get without trade. The question of which country gains the most from trade depends on whether one perceives gains in terms of absolute or relative measures. Notwithstanding, both countries clearly gain.

2.4 Introduction to the Heckscher-Ohlin Theorem and the Standard Trade Model

The next two trade models we discuss are the Heckscher-Ohlin Theorem and the Standard Trade Model. For each model we assume that the **Production Possibility Frontier (PPF)** is curvilinear as shown in Figure 4. This is a standard assumption and stems from the fact that there are diminishing returns on production for both of the goods X and Y. The implication is that when one good is produced in relatively high numbers (i.e., its production is close to the x- or y-axis) its marginal production beyond that level will be low, which makes substitution of the other item comparatively attractive. This has several purposes as we will describe in detail later. For now,

Figure 4. Benefits from trade and determining export and import

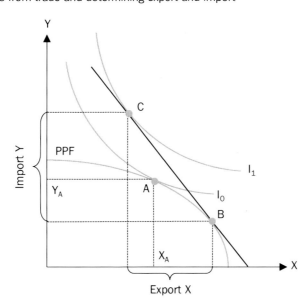

we use the same setup as described in the sections on Absolute and Comparative Advantages to explain how international trade can result in a win-win situation. Assume we are in a world with two goods, X and Y and that a country has a Production Possibility Frontier (PPF) whose equation is given by the curved line intersecting both the x- and y-axis. This line represents all potentially optimal production output combinations of goods X and Y. Without trade, production and consumption will occur at Point A since this is where the tangent to the PPF curve intersects the highest possible utility curve (I_0) to bring about the highest possible welfare for the country. The relative price of X to Y without trade, will be found as the slope of the vector which is perpendicular to the slope of the PPF's imaginary tangent to the indifference curve at Point A. With trade, however, prices will likely be different than without trade because different countries have different PPFs. In the graphical example, the relative price of X to Y is higher on the world market than on the home market, so the country produces at Point B rather than Point A. Following a classical microeconomics argument, this is because the country's budget constraint, along which it can trade in accordance with relative prices on the world market, begins at the point where its slope is tangent to the PPF. Because there is trading and X is more valuable than Y outside the home country, there will be more of X produced than Y compared to the situation prior to international trade. Finally, because world market prices are now accessible, the country can trade along its budget constraint slope and achieve consumption at Point C. This will enable it to reach a higher utility curve (I_1) and hence increase its welfare. This improvement will be realised as the country exports ($X_B - X_C$) and imports ($Y_C - Y_B$).

2.5   The Heckscher-Ohlin Theorem

We now turn our attention to the Heckscher-Ohlin Theorem. To describe its approach to international trade we begin by asking some simple questions: Why does Saudi Arabia export so much petrol and other petroleum-based products? Why is Côte d'Ivoire the world's largest exporter of cocoa? And why does Canada sell so many timber products to the United States? The answer is the same in each case: because they have a lot of crude oil, cocoa beans, and timber compared to their trading partners. Some economists might say these countries' international trade is a function of their input factors of production – in this case abundant natural resources – rather than resulting from comparative advantage. Others might argue that these countries have comparative advantages in these commodities precisely because they have access to input factors. Both sides would be right: there is more to global trade than a single-input model like Ricardo's comparative advantages is able to explain, despite its high degree of usefulness.

The Heckscher-Ohlin (H-O) Theorem is more versatile in that it assumes several input factors of production. Sometimes called a theory of **resource endowment**, this model considers resources to encompass far more than raw materials or labour, which makes it highly relevant in the modern world. As with any good economic model, the H-O Theorem builds its framework on a number of simplifying assumptions. This serves to direct the analysis' focus towards the main mechanisms of the model in order to understand how differences in relative resource endowments between nations can affect trade. The H-O is configured as a 2x2x2 model, meaning that there are two countries, two inputs of production, and two outputs in the form of products. For the sake of argument, we assume that the two countries are Home and Foreign, that the two inputs Capital (K) and Labour (L), and that the two outputs Computers and Cloth. We further assume that Home is relatively abundant in Capital but scarce in Labour, while the opposite true is for Foreign. Finally, we assume that the production of computers is relatively capital intensive and that the production of cloth is relatively labour intensive.

In simple terms, the H-O Theorem says that *if a country is abundant in a factor it should export the good whose production is intensive in that factor*. In our simplified case, it means that Home should export computers because it is abundant in capital, which computer production requires. Similarly, Foreign should export cloth since it is abundant in labour as cloth production demands.

In order to develop the model, we now assume two countries, two input factors, and two output factors, as before. The two countries vary only in relative resource endowments since they enjoy access to the same technology and education and have the same consumption preferences. The H-O model is designed to show how differences in relative resource endowments affect production and trade. The two input factors are capital and labour, and the two output factors vary in that the production of one is relatively capital intensive and the other relatively labour intensive. Meanwhile, Home is relatively capital abundant anond Foreign is relatively labour abundant. The capital-intensive product is computers and the labour-intensive product is cloth. Lastly, we assume that some resource substitution is possible between industries but not between countries. As a result, a country's Production Possibility Frontier (PPF) can be shown as a curved area which is skewed towards making the product which requires intensive amounts of the country's abundant factor. Home will therefore be biased towards computers and Foreign gear its production towards cloth (Figure 5). The PPF represents the possible production combinations wherein all available resources are used.

Figure 5. PPF for Home and Foreign

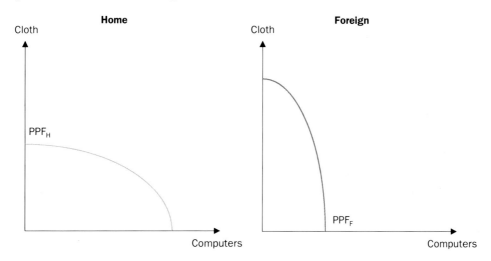

Without trade, each country will maximise utility by producing at the point on the PPF curve which is tangent to the highest possible utility curve (Figure 6). For Home this is Point A_H and for Foreign it is Point A_F. In each country, relative prices between the two goods will be determined by the line which is perpendicular to the slope of the tangent to both the PPF curve and the utility curve. This slope simultaneously represents the marginal substitution between input factors as well as output factors, which by microeconomics argument must equal the (inverse) relative prices. From Figure 6 it should be clear that the relative price of a computer in Home is lower than in Foreign, and vice versa for cloth. In other words, the product which is intensive in the abundant input factor is relatively cheaper than the product which is intensive in the scarce factor.

Figure 6. PPF, Utility Curves and Prices without Trade

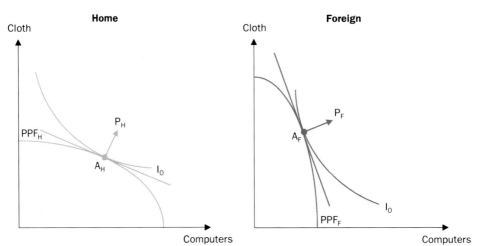

If trade is possible, then market mechanisms will clear the newly aggregated market by setting similar prices on similar products across countries. Ultimately, this will make the price of a computer the same in both Home and Foreign, just as it will for cloth. Naturally, this means that the higher prices of Home and Foreign products which relied on scarce resources before trade was possible will now decrease as they approach towards a single world market relative price. The same is true in reverse for prices which were lower in Home or Foreign due to the abundance of resource inputs in those areas: these prices will now rise.

With the new relative prices which prevail after Home and Foreign begin trading, each will find it optimal to produce more of the good which makes intensive use of its abundant input factor and less of the other product. Yet because trade is possible each country will export the product made from its abundant resource and import the other one. This will enable both countries to reach a higher utility curve and thus

Figure 7. PPF, Indifference Curves, and Prices after Trade

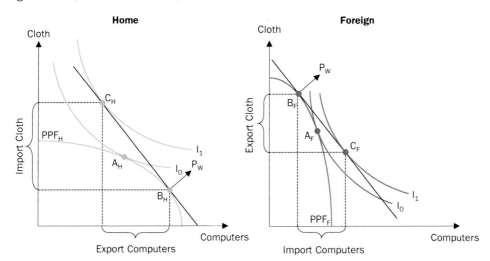

gain from trade as expected. This shift in production and trade is shown in Figure 7. It depicts the H-O Theorem graphically, showing that each country exports the product requiring intensive amounts of its abundant resource. An important consequence of this is that both countries specialise by producing more of the exported product and less of the imported one compared to the pre-trade situation.

In terms of accessing raw materials as an input for production and trade, the H-O Theorem predicts the outcome well. This is not at all surprising because Heckscher & Ohlin developed their model around this very observation when they analysed import and export trends from resource-rich vs. resource-poor countries around the world. The model takes this tenet a step further though by also claiming to be valid for input factors in general, especially labour and capital. Following the insight given by the model we would expect countries with abundant labour but scarce capital to export labour-intensive goods and import capital-intensive ones. By the same token, countries with abundant capital can be expected to export capital-intensive goods and import labour-intensive ones.

This is a powerful prediction and would seem to be easy to test empirically. After World War II the United States had far more capital than any other country in the world, so it would be expected, according to H-O Theorem logic, to export capital-intensive goods and import labour-intensive ones. However, in what came to be known as the Leontief Paradox, renowned Harvard economist Wassily Leontief found in 1953 that U.S. exports were in fact less capital-intensive that its imports, contrary to what the H-O Theorem predicted. A later study in 1962 by Harry P.

Bowen, Edward E. Leamer, and Leo Sveikaukas, involving 27 countries and 12 factors of production, confirmed the Leontief Paradox.

Several plausible explanations have been put forward to resolve this quandary where a strong theoretical result appears to have been violated in practice. One reason could be that the United States, with its highly developed post-war economy, had access to more advanced technology than its trading partners, which would violate the H-O Theorem's assumption of equal technology. A second reason could be that if the United States' economy was pursuing innovation through labour-intensive R&D activities, then the export of innovative products would be more likely. Once other countries adopted the technology and know-how required for wider production, these goods would become more capital-intensive, but at that point they would be exported to the U.S. A third explanation, which can be seen as a generalisation of the first two, is that the U.S. in particular, and capital-intensive countries in general, have a much more productive labour force because they have better education and technology. Therefore, if labour is not counted solely on a per-person basis but also includes a quality measure, the U.S. and other developed countries would be considered much more labour-intensive. Ultimately, the H-O Theorem predicts trade very well between regions for advanced countries like the U.S. and Japan, where technology and education levels are similar. Likewise, it has good predictive power when it comes to trade between developed and developing countries.

2.6   The Standard Trade Model

Combining Ricardo's comparative advantage with the Heckscher-Ohlin Theorem, a generalised or 'standardised' model can be developed which aids in understanding some general points about trade. Commonly referred to as *The Standard Trade Model*, this model does not assume specific characteristics of the production function as would be the case with both Ricardo and H-O; rather it uses the production possibility frontier (PPF) as its starting point without questioning how it emerges. In Ricardo's view, it would stem from specialisation and comparative advantages, whereas H-O would explain its genesis in terms of resource endowments. In any event the Standard Trade Model utilises a supply-side perspective to analyse the impact of economic growth on relative supply and demand and, consequently, on relative prices. This in turn ultimately leads to changes in society's welfare and income distribution levels. The fact that the analysis' measures are relative, rather than absolute, means that they represent the supply, demand, and price of one good divided by the other, rather than the absolute values themselves.

With this background in place, we use the same PPF as given in the H-O Theorem. However, the model no longer needs to reflect different resource endowments between countries. It *could* reflect them, but this is no longer a requirement because the model can now consider Ricardian comparative advantages as well. The main point is that the PPF is curvilinear because of diminishing marginal returns, as discussed previously. As before, we define two countries – Home and Foreign – each making two products, computers and cloth. Home is again biased towards production of computers, while Foreign is biased towards cloth (Figure 8).

Figure 8. PPFs in Home and Foreign

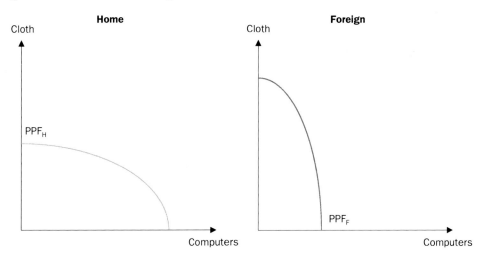

With international trade occurring, we have a world market price (P_w) as depicted in Figure 9. For this example, we define P_w as the price of computers in terms of cloth (relative price of computers to cloth). Stated differently, we determine the relative price of a computer by how many pieces of cloth it takes to buy one on the international markets. Meanwhile, relative supply and demand refer to how many computers are being produced or demanded in terms of pieces of cloth. Finally, the relative world price will be the price that clears the world markets for both computers and cloth (Figure 9). It is worth noticing that because the model uses only relative terms, the market mechanisms and equilibrium are also expressed in this way. Figure 9 therefore shows that when moving down along the Relative Demand (RD) curve, the relative demand of computers to cloth increases as the relative price of computers to cloth declines. Following the same logic for supply, when the relative price of computers increases their relative supply will increase in tandem. The equilibrium point is therefore found where both relative price and relative production clear the world market.

Trade is not only about prices and quantities; it is also concerned with change. Innovation happens every day as companies, industries, and countries constantly seek to gain competitive advantages one way or another in order to grow their businesses or expand the economy as a whole. In the Standard Trade Model growth occurs as the PPF expands outwards, making room for more production with the same input factors. There are four distinct ways growth can occur as we will see shortly in Table 4, each with a slightly different effect on prices and welfare. Regardless of the type of growth a country experiences, however, it is most often biased towards a specific industry, sector, or product. Very rarely, if ever, is it spread evenly across an entire country's production. Under the Standard Trade Model's framework, the key consideration for trade is whether an economy's growth is biased towards exports or imports and whether it occurs in Home or Foreign.

One type of growth, export-biased Home growth, is depicted in Figure 10. In relative terms we see that Home's productivity in computers has risen more than its productivity in cloth. Because the relative supply of computers increases due to productivity gains, its relative price will decrease as shown in the relative supply curve's shift to the right, from RS_0 to RS_1. Home will therefore produce and export

Figure 9. Relative Supply and Demand

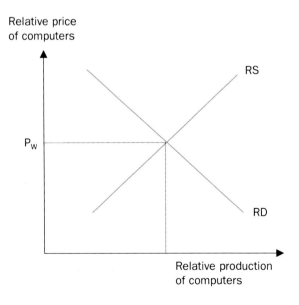

more computers, while Foreign will produce fewer computers and more cloth, as shown in the lower two panels of Figure 10.

In the case of Home's export-biased growth, the price of exports relative to imports decreases. The price of exports divided by the price of imports is called **the Terms of Trade (ToT)**. The usefulness of ToT is that it allows us to analyse the aggregated welfare effects from biased growth and understand conclusively who the trade's winners and losers are. Under the export-biased growth scenario shown in Figure 10, ToT will decrease (worsen) for Home but increase (improve) for Foreign. When ToT decreases for a given country its economy worsens, all other things being

Figure 10. Export-Biased Growth in Home

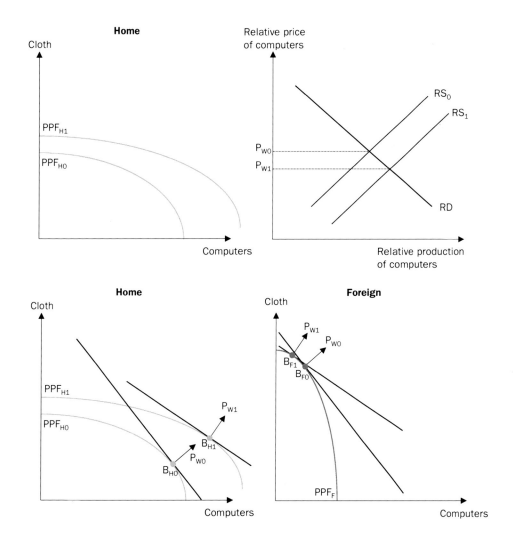

equal, because it sells its products at lower relative prices and hence generates less income for same quantity of exports. This in turn will lead to lower consumption and welfare for the nation as a whole, if we assume that the world market clears all prices due to perfectly competitive markets. Table 4 below, and its associated descriptions, expand the discussion to cover all four types of growth, as well as demonstrate the net welfare effects. It is noteworthy that export-biased growth has a positive effect on a country's welfare because any growth means higher productivity, but paradoxically, these higher exports worsen its ToT since the equilibrium price declines. As a result, the country must export more units in order to maintain the same level of welfare. The four different types of growth, and their welfare effects on Home and Foreign, are shown in Table 4 below.

Table 4. Welfare Effects from Biased Growth

	Terms of Trade (Home)	Terms of Trade (Foreign)	Home Welfare Effect from Growth (Volume Effect)	Home Welfare Effect from Terms of Trade (Price Effect)	Foreign Welfare Effect from Growth (Volume Effect)	Foreign Welfare Effect from Terms of Trade (Price Effect)
Home Export-biased Growth	-	+	+	-	N/A	+
			Net effect: +/(-*)		Net effect: +	
Home Import- biased Growth	+	-	+	+	N/A	-
			Net effect: +		Net effect: -	
Foreign Export- biased Growth	+	-	N/A	+	+	-
			Net effect: +		Net effect: +/(-*)	
Foreign Import-Biased Growth	-	+	N/A	-	+	+
			Net effect: -		Net effect: +	

* If the net welfare effect from export biased growth is negative it is known as 'immiserising growth'.

Table 4 shows that regardless of which type of growth a country experiences, it is likely to become wealthier even though the income distribution within society may change. Yet, paradoxically, theoretical analysis and empirical evidence show that when a country experiences export-biased growth it can actually end up poorer. This is known as **immiserising growth** and will be explored in greater depth along with the more intuitive and common effects of growth.

In the case of Home's export-biased immiserising growth, its welfare will decrease. The negative effect from worsened ToT more than outweighs the positive effect from increased production volumes. Therefore, the net income effect, and consequently the welfare effect, end up being negative. This is illustrated in Figure 11 where consumption after growth takes place on a lower utility curve compared to before growth, which implies lower welfare. Note that immiserising growth can only occur when a country's export-biased growth is large enough to influence world market prices.

In the case of Home export-biased growth without immiserising growth, Home will experience higher income due to higher volumes of both products, despite the negative effect of worsened ToT. Higher income causes consumption to take place along a higher utility curve, thereby improving overall welfare. Foreign will experience higher welfare because of improved ToT.

Finally, in the case of Home import-biased growth, Home will experience higher welfare both because of higher volumes and improved ToT. Foreign, however, will suffer from lowered welfare because its ToT are worsened.

Setting aside the special case of immiserising growth, one difference between the export- and import-biased growth scenarios described above is that with the former, Home improves its comparative advantage, whereas with the latter it does not (although its welfare improves). A second difference is that with Home's export-biased growth, Foreign's comparative advantage improves and therefore enables it to purchase and consume more. This is why positive net effects are seen in both countries as a result of this type of growth. On the other hand, when Home gets better at producing cloth (import-biased growth), which is outside its comparative advantage, Foreign loses some of its comparative advantage in relative terms due to worsened Terms of Trade and thus experiences lower welfare. Immiserising growth, mean-

Figure 11. Immiserising Home export-biased growth

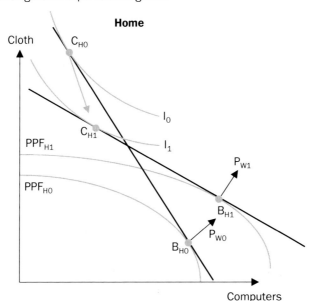

while, demonstrates the way in which too much growth from specialisation in a single industry can be risky because, on balance, it may lead to lower welfare.

In a competitive globalised world, Terms of Trade (ToT) is an important concept because it captures the essence of a nation's competitiveness. When ToT improve a country can sell its product at relatively higher prices, which in turn increases its income. This ultimately allows it to consume more and thus advance to a higher utility curve where it enjoys a higher level of welfare. The country receives the combined benefits of higher prices for its exports along with access to cheaper imported goods.

The special case of immiserising growth demonstrates the way in which large countries can worsen their economic situation by specialising too much. In a competitive world prices follow the dictates of supply and demand, so prices will fall as supply rises. Therefore, if a large export-biased country expands its economy by producing cheaper and cheaper goods it must ensure that the increased production volume compensates for a lower profit per unit. Otherwise its domestic welfare will decline through lower income even as the rest of the world enjoys the benefits of lower prices and increases its consumption possibilities. In our world today, e.g. China may be at risk of immiserising growth since it specialises in producing inexpensive goods which it sells to the rest of the world at highly competitive prices. These prices increase welfare in the United States and Europe, for instance, as people buy 'Made in China' products and see their paychecks stretch further. In China, however, ultra-competitive prices may lower manufacturing margins in a way that higher sales volumes do not compensate for, which, on balance, puts the nation's welfare at risk even as its economy expands.

2.7   Economies of Scale

Up until now, with the possible exception of Mercantilism, a fundamental assumption of the models has been that of competitive markets. This implies that the industry or nation which is most competitive will have the most favourable circumstances for production. In general, these circumstances stem from two sources, comparative advantages and resource endowments. Comparative advantages arise from the higher labour productivity which technology makes possible – also known as specialisation. Resource endowments, however, are bestowed by nature or acquired through investments in human capital, technology, or machinery.

Modern trade theories do not overlook the important insights of the Ricardian and H-O models but rather add another dimension. Instead of assuming perfect competition, they consider that competition and markets are often imperfect. Moreover, modern economic theory also considers that a country's production can be scalable and that network effects often add value to international trade. In general, these modifications are known as Economies of Scale (EoS) and are said to be in force when unit costs decrease as output rises (Figure 12). There are four distinct types of EoS, which we now turn our attention to in detail: Internal, External, and Dynamic EoS, and Economies of *Scope*.

Figure 12. Economies of Scale

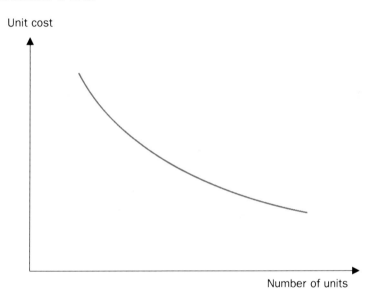

Internal EoS occurs when a single firm enjoys economies of scale. **External EoS**, meanwhile, applies to an industry as a whole. When the entire industry benefits from lower unit costs, the reasons are typically quite different from those which make Internal EoS possible. **Dynamic EoS**, for its part, is also known as the experience curve and refers to the fact that the more production units a company manufactures over a product's lifetime the cheaper it can produce additional units, due to experience in production. Finally, **Economies of Scope** refers to a phenomenon where the broader a company's range of products is, the cheaper it can be to produce and sell each unit. With this introduction we now move on to a more detailed description of these four economies of scale.

2.7.1 Internal Economies of Scale

First, we consider **Internal Economies of Scale**, which occur when a single firm enjoys a cost advantage due to its size. The automobile industry provides a good example. Its firms are characterised by multi-billion-dollar operations with sprawling production facilities and large fixed costs that include design engineering, assembly line tooling, quality control, and marketing, among others. Obviously, the more cars a single manufacturer can produce and sell, the more units it has available for amortising these fixed costs.

If we turn our attention to Denmark, we see that despite being a small nation it is home to some of the largest firms in the world in selected industries. For example, one of the largest container ship and supply vessel firms, A.P. Moller – Maersk, is headquartered in Copenhagen, while Vestas Wind Systems dominates the global wind turbine space. Also, Novo Nordisk is one of the top pharmaceuticals in insulin while Oticon, Widex, and ReSound are three of the six largest hearing aid manufacturers in the world. Finally, there is Lego, whose products are known and loved by children around the world. All of these firms enjoy Internal EoS because they have large fixed costs which can be amortised over sales.

For Maersk, this fixed cost is the container ships whichh convey its customers' goods across the oceans. For Vestas, Novo Nordisk, Oticon, Widex, and ReSound it is not so much about capital equipment like factories or ships as it is about research and development (R&D). In fact, the renewable energy, pharmaceutical, and medical device industries are all characterised by high R&D costs which allow participants to stay at the forefront of knowledge acquisition. Because this knowledge is proprietary and therefore protected by patents and licenses, when one firm develops a breakthrough technology or discovers a promising new drug it receives a competitive advantage vis-à-vis other firms which it benefits from by producing and selling as many units as possible. Lego, meanwhile, also has large fixed costs, but these are not concentrated in capital equipment or technology development. Rather, they involve market research and brand promotion expenditures throughout the world. Lego wants to understand how children play, what their development patterns are, and how to predict and capitalise upon the 'next big thing'. Thanks to their investments in marketing intelligence and branding they do this better than almost anyone else. In 2016 they became the world's biggest toy manufacturer, in large part because of the unique insights which their Internal EoS made possible.

Each of these examples involve Danish companies engaging in imperfect competition – specifically oligopolistic competition where they have a prominent position in a global market dominated by a few large firms. In general, imperfect competition will either be oligopolistic, monopolistic, or involve a monopoly. Monopolistic competition is characterised by many small firms producing and selling a related but slightly differentiated product. These firms do not enjoy large economies of scale, so they tend to operate as small entities on a mostly local basis. Examples include restaurants, bars, coffee shops, grocery stores, etc., which are usually single-location businesses often with a physical brick-and-mortar structure. Even though they are small they still have the potential to contribute significantly to international trade. Monopolies, as well, could certainly be involved in global trade, but there are not many of them in practice since they are often prohibited by law. The main types of businesses in international trade are therefore oligopolies, which, as mentioned, consist of a few large companies which compete on a national or international scale. We provided several examples of Danish companies engaged in global competition, but of course there are others in Denmark and countless more around the world. Airlines, technology companies, biotech firms, beer and soft drink bottlers, cocoa processors, investment banks, and many more exist in industries where large fixed costs cause unit costs to decrease as a function of sales volume.

2.7.2 External Economies of Scale

External Economies of Scale are concerned with the efficiency of whole industries. For example, why is Silicon Valley the place to go when you are a high-tech company, and especially if you are a start-up? Why are New York City and London such powerhouses in global finance? Why is Detroit known as the Motor City? At first glance it would seem that industries or business clusters in a certain geographical area would make competition between firms fiercer than if they were more scattered, but competition is not the issue here – the availability of resource inputs is, along with industry knowledge and labour sharing. Competition over production output is not a significant issue in a globalised world, but what about competition on inputs? For example, is it difficult for a company to compete against an entire industry when it wants to hire someone, instead of being the only business around to offer a specific type of job? Not at all. On the contrary, clusters attract skilled labour and specialised suppliers, so if a business owner wants access to this pool of resource inputs, he or she needs to be where they are. In addition, because of labour pooling, supplier specialisation, and networking, there is a high degree of information sharing within a business cluster. We now explore in greater depth these three main drivers of external economies of scale.

1) **Labour market pooling**. This is good for both employees and firms in that it affords access to jobs and labour simultaneously. When employees and firms are spread across a region, significant changes in the business environment can have

a dramatic negative impact. Imagine a firm with rapid sales growth that cannot find qualified employees. Growth would stall and the firm would begin to lose strategic opportunities. Its balance sheet might even be compromised if continued growth were needed to support large capital expenditure's payback. When a large labour force is accessible, though, hiring new people is only a matter of paying the right wages, not a matter of finding them. Now imagine the opposite situation, where a firm is downsizing its operations or closing. If the company is the only one of its kind in the area, its employees may well have to move far away to find a new job, with significant consequences for uprooted families. With a large pool of firms, though, workers can find new jobs much more quickly and easily. In both cases, labour pooling solves a crucial problem and facilitates a well-functioning labour market, in addition to knowledge sharing and innovation.

2) **Specialised suppliers**. Specialised suppliers provide important inputs to their industry and are often strategically located near the cluster to provide just-in-time delivery and on-site customer support. Examples include suppliers of equipment requiring unique expertise and know-how, purveyors of specialised infrastructure, customised market or product knowledge, and schools and universities which provide education tailored to the industry's needs. Often-times these suppliers also serve as repositories of industry knowledge which can aid innovation and provide new ideas for solving problems or connecting subject matter experts to one another.

3) **Knowledge Sharing**. Both labour market pooling and specialised suppliers facilitate information sharing for industries with external EoS. From a competitive point of view, this may appear to be bad for business, particularly for firms which do not receive shared information. Aside from the priority to safeguard confidential information, it is much cheaper for an industry to develop and share information than it is for a single firm because the acquisition cost is spread across a wider base. Moreover, industry best practices will be 'stress tested' to ensure robustness, given that they will be utilised in many environments and subjected to a wide variety of real-world applications. Finally, acquiring the knowledge necessary for innovation and continuous improvement seems to happen more efficiently when the people involved interact socially, whether outside the job or at industry conferences and events, while the companies themselves are sharpened through interaction with their peers. All in all, clusters acquire knowledge better than single firms.

In Denmark, although A.P. Moller-Maersk is one of the biggest container shipping company in the world, in fact there are several other large merchant marine players as well, making the country an important node in the worldwide shipping industry. Also contributing to this industry is Copenhagen Business School, which offers a number of courses with a specific maritime focus, as well as a Ph.D. program. Furthermore, until recently one of the world's biggest shipyards was located in Denmark, and a number of mid-sized shipbuilders remain. In other words, external economies of scale make Denmark a good place for maritime companies to locate, and this fact is recognised around the world. In recent years the Danish wind turbine industry with Vestas as its flagship, has also begun to benefit from external economies of scale. Access to these economies was the main reason Vestas' German competitor, Siemens-Gamesa entered Denmark in 2007 and it now carries out a substantial part of its production and equipment transport operations at its facility less than two hours away from Vestas. Similarly, Ørsted (former DONG), who is the pioneer and world leader in offshore wind turbine farms is headquartered only an hour away, which among other benefits facilitates knowledge sharing. In another example, it is no coincidence that three of the world's six largest hearing aid companies – Oticon, Widex, and ReSound – are located in Denmark. In short, firms of all sizes are often well-positioned to enjoy external EoS when clusters are created.

It is sometimes argued that governments should support **infant industries** which have the potential to achieve large external economies of scale in the long run. Since there are no economies of scale when the industry is small, the government should nurse and support the small industry, the logic goes, even create demand for it, in an effort to stimulate its growth. This type of 'unfair' competition is often not well received internationally, and it is even illegal in the European Union. One example of a Danish industry whichh could be said to have received governmental support is the wind turbine industry from the 1970s - 1990s. This was done through various subsidies which included, among other things, a state-guaranteed minimum payment per kWh to the owners of wind turbines. Today, however, Vestas and the industry as a whole are well able to stand on their own. Elsewhere, Korean shipyards have been accused of receiving subsidies from the state which have now made them among the largest, most capable shipbuilders in the world. Finally, and perhaps most notably, are the many Chinese state-owned oligopolies which benefit from a lack of foreign competition because the government restricts access to the domestic Chinese market.

2.7.3 Dynamic Economies of Scale

Dynamic Economies of Scale refers to the experience curve. Whereas regular economies of scale cause unit costs to decrease as a function of greater volumes, the experience curve shows how unit costs decrease as a function of total aggregated production over time. The more units in total that a firm produces over a given product's lifespan, the more experience it acquires in these units' manufacture. This, in turn, will lead to lower production costs in the future. The experience curve looks much like the well-known unit cost curve which exists for EoS (Figure 12), with the difference being that the horizontal axis shows aggregated production over the years. A final note is that the experience curve is different from the learning curve, in that the learning curve specifically refers to labour efficiency as a function of repetition. The experience curve takes the labour efficiency effect into account alongside the effects of specialisation, standardisation, resource allocation, R&D, and technology.

2.7.4 Economies of Scope

Economies of Scope are achieved when unit costs decrease as a function of broader product offerings. They often exist at companies with Internal or External EoS, but the type of economy is different in that it reduces the cost of bringing goods to market. One example of a firm with economies of scope is the Danish global brewer, Carlsberg, whose product portfolio contains more than 100 different types and brands of beer. Although these beers are not produced in the same facility, Carlsberg achieves economies of scope because its network and distribution channels enable it to reduce the cost of raw materials, shared services, and logistics. Another firm which illustrates this dynamic is the Swedish furniture retailer, IKEA. Thanks to its attractive modern designs and affordable pricing, it has become the world's largest furniture seller, and it achieves economies of scope through its selling channels. In particular, as customers enter one its cavernous trademark stores, the broad selection of appealing home goods and furniture captures their imagination and they leave with more purchases than they originally intended.

2.8   Michael Porter's Diamond Model

Harvard economist and Professor Michael Porter is internationally renowned for developing the 1979 strategy framework known as Porter's Five Forces, which bears his name. In 1990, though, he also published an article in the Harvard Business Review about the competitive advantages of nations and proposed a framework called the Diamond Model (Figure 13). He claimed that his findings differ dramatically from other well-established theories, but there appear to be many resemblances between his model and those presented in this chapter. To conduct our own analysis, we cite Porter's words from the introduction to his article:

'National prosperity is created, not inherited. It does not grow out of a country's natural endowments, its labour pool, its interest rates, or its currency's value, as classical economics insists.

A nation's competitiveness depends on the capacity of its industry to innovate and upgrade. Companies gain advantage against the world's best competitors because of pressure and challenge. They benefit from having strong domestic rivals, aggressive home-based suppliers, and demanding local customers.

In a world of increasingly global competition, nations have become more, not less, important. As the basis of competition has shifted more and more to the creation and assimilation of knowledge, the role of the nation has grown. Competitive advantage is created and sustained through a highly localised process. Differences in national values, culture, economic structures, institutions, and histories all contribute to competitive success. There are striking differences in the patterns of competitiveness in every country; no nation can or will be competitive in every or even most industries. Ultimately, nations succeed in particular industries because their home environment is the most forward-looking, dynamic, and challenging.'

Porter's research on the source of a nation's competitiveness has never received the same attention as his work on strategy,[3] but his premise nonetheless provides a useful framework for understanding why nations pursue different industries and technologies in their quest for competitive advantage. In short, the Diamond Model points to four factors which, when taken together, determine the competitiveness of a nation. In Porter's words, these are described as follows:

1. Factor Conditions: the nation's position in factors of production, such as skilled labour or infrastructure, necessary to compete in a given industry.
2. Demand Conditions: the nature of home-market demand for the industry's product or service.
3. Related and Supporting Industries: the presence or absence in the nation of supplier industries and other related industries that are internationally competitive.
4. Firm Strategy, Structure, and Rivalry: the conditions in the nation governing how companies are created, organised, and managed, as well as the nature of domestic rivalry.

Factor Conditions. According to Porter, the idea that labour, land, natural resources, capital, and infrastructure comprise important factors, '*is at best incomplete and at worst incorrect.*' Nations do not inherit but create the most important factors. '*Denmark has two hospitals that concentrate in studying and treating diabetes—and a world leading export position in insulin. Holland has premier research institutes in the cultivation, packaging, and shipping of flowers, where it is the world's export leader. The most important factors of production are those that involve sustained and heavy investment and are special-*

---

3. See Porter's Five Forces and the Value Chain frameworks.

Figure 13. The Diamond Model

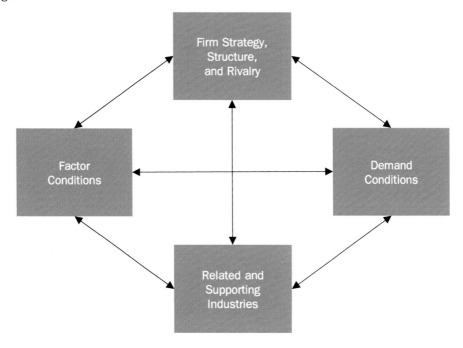

ised.' Meanwhile, labour and capital can be accessed through a global strategy or substituted through technology. *'Highly specialised ... factors are scarcer, more difficult for foreign competitors to imitate – and they require sustained investment to create.'*

Porter further argues that selective disadvantages in basic factors can become advantages through innovation.[4] The Japanese statement, *'We are an island nation with no natural resources,'* reflects the understanding that these deficiencies have only served to spur their competitive innovation. Meanwhile, the technologically advanced steel mini-mills in and around Brescia, Italy, were the result of initial disadvantages in regard to high capital costs, high energy costs, and a lack of local raw materials. To quite Porter, *'they converted factor disadvantages into competitive advantage.'*

Demand Conditions. *'It might seem that the globalisation of competition would diminish the importance of home demand,'* Porter argues. On the contrary, though, home markets have a disproportionate effect on how companies perceive and interpret demand.

---

4. As the saying goes, *'Necessity is the mother of invention.'*

However, it is not necessarily the size of the home market as much as the character of home demand which determines its impact. *'Sweden's long-standing concern for handicapped people has spawned an increasingly competitive industry focused on special needs. Denmark's environmentalism has led to success for companies in water-pollution control equipment and windmills [wind turbines].'*

Related and Supporting Industries.[5] Competitive home-based suppliers deliver cost-effective inputs in an *'efficient, early, rapid, and sometimes preferential way.'* More important though are the advantages which *'supporting industries provide in innovation and upgrading—an advantage based on close working relationships.'* Related and supporting industries gain further advantage through efficient communication, information sharing, R&D collaboration, upgraded technology, and innovation and new skills. *'The Swiss success in pharmaceuticals emerged out of previous international success in the dye industry, for example; Japanese dominance in electronic musical keyboards grows out of success in acoustic instruments combined with a strong position in consumer electronics.'*

Firm Strategy, Structure, and Rivalry. *'The presence of strong local rivals is a final, and powerful, stimulus to the creation and persistence of competitive advantage. This is true of small countries, like Switzerland, where the rivalry among its pharmaceutical companies, Hoffmann-La Roche, Ciba-Geigy, and Sandoz, contributes to a leading worldwide position. It is true in the United States in the computer and software industries. Nowhere is the role of fierce rivalry more apparent than in Japan, where there are 112 companies competing in machine tools, 34 in semiconductors, 25 in audio equipment, 15 in cameras – in fact, there are usually double figures in the industries in which Japan boasts global dominance. Among all the points on the diamond, domestic rivalry is arguably the most important because of the powerfully stimulating effect it has on all the others.'*

Two additional factors are often emphasised in more recent Diamond Models, which are the roles of **Government** and **Chance** (Figure 14). While Porter talks about the role of Government in the article without explicitly referring to it as a factor, Chance can be considered as the residual element of competitive positioning which the other factors cannot explain. This makes for a MECE[6] analysis which is capable of capturing any explanation.

---

5. Note that this is equivalent to External EoS.
6. Mutually Exclusive Combined Exhaustive. MECE frameworks are often used in consultancy in order to make sure to take in all information without double counting.

Figure 14. The Extended Diamond Model

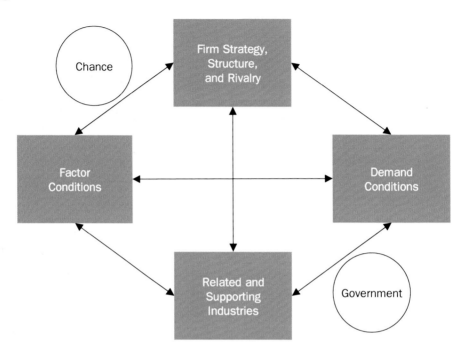

According to Porter, Government should work as a catalyst and challenger to create favourable underlying conditions in the diamond. It is not Government's role to create competitive industries, this should rather be left to companies. Successful governments are those which create an environment where companies can gain competitive advantage, rather than involve themselves directly in industry through nationalion and operating State-Owned Enterprises (SOEs). Although an exception may sometimes be necessary when industries are in the early development stage,[7] the general principle is that governments should play an indirect rather than direct role. *'Japan's government, at its best, understands this role better than anyone—including the point that nations pass through stages of competitive development and that government's appropriate role shifts as the economy progresses. By stimulating early demand for advanced products, confronting industries with the need to pioneer frontier technology through symbolic cooperative projects, establishing prizes that reward quality, and pursuing other policies that magnify the forces of the diamond, the Japanese government accelerates the pace of innovation.'*

7. Note that this is equivalent to the infant industries argument.

2.9   The Product Space Conditions the Development of Nations

The Product Space Framework (C.A. Hidalgo, B. Klinger, A.-L. Barabási, R. Hausmann; 2007) was developed through collaboration between four researchers from various universities, including MIT and Harvard. The idea was first published in *Science* in 2007 but has since received considerable attention from economic researchers and policymakers alike because it helps explain why some economies undergo steady growth while others are unable to develop.

The Product Space Framework is an empirical model which describes the correlation of trade between 775 product categories in each country of the world. The model's output is a network of connections between these product categories which can be represented as a 775x775 matrix or in graphical format as shown in Figure 1. The framework shows that there is a strict correlation between certain types of products, suggesting that a country cannot simply begin manufacturing a certain item if it is not already producing related goods. In the article introducing the Product Space Framework the authors use the analogy of a forest and monkeys to explain this correlation and describe the notion of a product space.

Imagine that a product is a tree and the set of all products is a forest. The firms in a country can be likened to a group of monkeys living in trees throughout the forest, which is to say, they are manufacturing different products. As the authors state, *'The process of growth implies moving from a poorer part of the forest, where trees have little fruit, to better parts of the forest.'* In order to grow, the monkeys need to jump to new trees, and firms, by extension, must deploy human, physical, and institutional capital. Whereas traditional growth theory assumes there is always a nearby tree, the Product Space acknowledges that the forest's trees are sometimes scattered over large areas and that monkeys cannot move freely to any new place they choose. In the real world, likewise, countries cannot randomly develop new products but must rather already produce related products or have industries in place from which to build them. Consequently, *'The structure of this space and a country's orientation within it become of great importance to the development of countries.'*

A variety of factors may cause relatedness between products, which is akin to the closeness between trees. Examples could be the intensity of labour required, or land, capital, technology, supply chains, and institutions. The product space takes an agnostic approach and looks only at correlation, not causation. This is what makes it an empirical model, rather than a theoretical one. The authors therefore use an outcome-based measure, one which determines 'proximity' and measures the degree of **relatedness** between two products, which we detail in the following paragraph. For example, a country which exports apples will probably have the capability to export pears as well. It would have the soil, climate, skilled labour, and packing technology required for apples which could easily be expanded to pears. Copper wires and the manufacture of home appliance, on the other hand, do not seem to have many factors in common. Proximity is therefore the concept that captures this relationship.

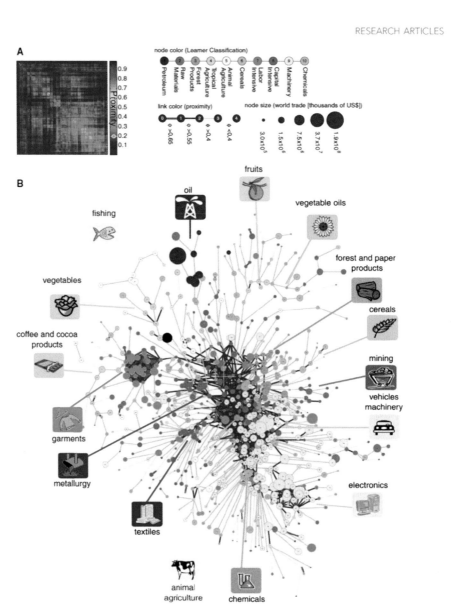

Fig. 1. The product space. **(A)** Hierarchically clustered proximity (φ) matrix representing the 775 SITC-4 product classes exported in the 1998–2000 period. **(B)** Network representation of the product space. Links are color coded with their proximity value. The sizes of the nodes are proportional to world trade, and their colors are chosen according to the classification introduced by Leamer.

Fig. 2. Localization of the productive structure for different regions of the world. The products for which the region has an *RCA* > 1 are denoted by black squares.

In order to measure proximity between product categories, the article introduces an important concept known as **Revealed Comparative Advantage (RCA$_{c,i}$)**. *RCA$_{c,i}$ measures whether a country c exports more of good i, as a share of its total exports than the 'average' country',* such that it has RCA > 1, rather than RCA < 1). **Proximity** can therefore be defined as the probability that a country will develop an RCA in a certain product (*i*), given that it actually has an RCA in another product (*j*). The higher the probability, the higher the proximity, and thus the more closely the products are related. Having defined these concepts, the article goes on to describe the consequences of trade patterns in different parts of the world, as depicted in Figure 2.

Figure 2 shows the pattern of specialisation for four regions in the product space. Products exported with RCA > 1 are shown as black squares. Industrialised countries occupy the core, which consist of machinery, metal products, and chemicals but they also involved in some of the more peripheral products such as textiles, forest products, and animal agriculture. East Asian countries are more specialised in garments, electronics, and textiles, while Latin America and the Caribbean are further out on the periphery in mining, agriculture, and garments. Finally, sub-Saharan Africa exports only a few product types, all of which are on the far periphery of the product space. Taken together, we see that each region of the world has a noticeable pattern of specialisation within the Product Space Framework which in turn outlines the parameters for its countries' overall development.

2.10 Concluding remarks

As we close this chapter, we have seen that trade theories and models seek to describe how nations gain competitive advantages over one another. Mercantilism was concerned with empires exploiting their colonies to accumulate as much wealth as possible. Adam Smith and David Ricardo were less confrontational in their approach in that they suggested that nations build competitive advantages through specialisation. The Heckscher-Ohlin Theorem and the Standard Trade Model did not recommend an approach to building competitive advantage, but they analysed the consequences of initial resource endowments and changes in the Production Possibility Frontiers. Finally, Economies of Scale, Porter's Diamond Model and the Product Space Framework are based on empirical observations and models which describe the reasons for competitiveness and trade composition rather than theorise about them. Historically, trade theories have tended to focus on the competitiveness between countries, and later on a narrower scope of focus on industries and firms. Today, however, with the unbundling of the global supply chain into individual tasks, macroeconomic theorists no longer seek to develop new ground-breaking philoso-phies of trading. Rather, they strive to identify and explain the patterns of interna-tional trade which are seen in the world we live in – a world which, up to the present day, has become increasingly more globalised.

CHAPTER 3

Trade Barriers

Trade barriers can best be understood from a mercantilist approach where the goal is to boost exports and reduce imports in a way that maximises a specific country's trade balance. In general, this protectionist approach to global trade contradicts the free trade argument that if all nations specialise in producing according to their comparative advantage each will benefit on balance. As we saw in Chapter 1, the premise of free trade has gained widespread support since the end of World War II and trade policies have been conducted within international frameworks. The first of these was developed in 1947 and was known as the General Agreement of Trade and Tariffs (GATT); the second, which replaced it in 1995 is called the World Trade Organization (WTO).

Notwithstanding the stability given by 70 years of free international trade, mercantilist arguments and protectionist measures are a part of *realpolitik* and have gained a certain degree of political traction in recent years. To understand the implications, we delve into the primary classical arguments brought forward when arguing in favour of protectionist policies.

Protection of jobs is a pervasive argument when dynamic changes in global competition shift production from one country to another and lead to long-time workers suddenly finding themselves displaced. If these workers' transition to other sectors of the economy is slow or if the loss of jobs is readily observable and captures the media's attention, arguments for protecting struggling industries can gain political currency, especially if the impacted industries are well-organised and carry significant weight in the economy.

A related rationale proffered by protectionists is that **anti-dumping measures** are needed to protect against cheap foreign labour. Here, the claim is that domestic industries are unable to compete with lower salaries abroad and that these salaries constitute social dumping which domestic workers should be shielded from. This argument falls short, however, in that it fails to adjust for differences in productivity. In particular, wage levels ought to be higher in Germany, for instance, than in Kenya because a German factory will usually be more capital-intensive and therefore more efficient than a Kenyan one. Theoretically, the Heckscher-Olin factor endowment model discussed in Chapter 2 would suggest that with more global trade and inter-dependence, resource payments tend to equalise between countries over time, which leads to downward pressure on wages in a developed country and increased wages in emerging markets.

A third argument put forward is the need to **level the playing field.** Some foreign governments give preferential treatment to their domestic industries, perhaps by permitting lax environmental standards, light regulatory burdens, low taxation, industry subsidies, and inadequate worker protection laws. This makes it difficult or impossible for foreign companies to compete, protectionist-minded people say, so import tariffs should be imposed on their products to create a fair and level playing field where all competitors are equal.

A fourth argument is the **infant-industry** approach which we discussed previously in Chapter 2. In this case governments seek to protect new domestic producers by restricting imports so that local production and capacity can be built up through protectionism and, in the long run, reduce their dependence on foreign technology and capital.

A fifth argument is **national security** concerns. A country may claim that its national security is at stake if it requires large amounts of a vital good which it could not produce enough of in the event of war, thus making it dependent on imports which could potentially be cut off.

A sixth reason for protectionist rhetoric is that threatening other countries with trade restrictions can be used as a **bargaining tool.** The goal is to force a country's trading partners to re-negotiate trade deals and possibly remove or reduce restrictions, ideally leading to freer trade. The problem is that if this strategy fails the

De-globalisation in Russia

Since 2014, Russia has, in effect, been de-globalising its economy, using the rationale that reducing imports will promote domestic growth through import substitution. This is an example of the infant industry argument: if a domestic industry is on the verge of being competitive, protectionist policies will allow it to catch up with, and then outpace, its international competitors. As a general rule, however, a promising industry which lags behind foreign competitors will often rely on state-of-the-art technology which must be imported. Second, the protected industries need to approach world-class productivity rates in order to be truly competitive, but in Russia labour productivity – especially in protected industries – lags behind that of the U.S. or Europe. Third, in order to catch up, the so-called infant industry must be able to sell to a large domestic market. While Russia is a large country, its domestic market is not significant, especially given the recent impact of lower oil prices. Russia's share of world GDP is approximately 1.6%, or roughly the size of Spain or Canada. Finally, whatever protection is imposed must be temporary or else the protected industry will lack incentives to catch up with the rest of the world.

country must either implement the tariff and face potential retaliation or back down with a loss of negotiating leverage.

A seventh and final argument given by protectionist-minded governments is that trade barriers can prevent a potential **offshore tipping point** from being reached for entire industries. The logic is that clusters of companies often concentrate in a specific locale due to external economies of scale as discussed in Chapter 2. Offshore tipping points may occur when there are economies of scale abroad or a reduced availability of domestic skilled workers, and once companies leave it is difficult to bring them back.

China offers an interesting case study in regard to offshore tipping points. Because it is a lower cost manufacturing country with an increasingly skilled labour force, it offers significant benefits to production-oriented companies. This attractiveness causes an increase in FDI inflows to China as new manufacturing companies enter, which in turn promotes the clustering of industries within China. This creation of external economies of scale then allows companies to sell products at a lower cost, which ultimately benefits consumers around the world while generating more revenue and income for the companies as export demand increases. In the long run this dynamic allows China's manufacturing industry to acquire significant know-how and attain world-class productivity levels.

Meanwhile, if the United States, for example, sees many of its production-oriented companies leave its shores for China, its manufacturing base could see a gradual de-clustering and lose some of its economies of scale. Ultimately, this will shape the pattern of international trade (Krugman, Obstfeld and Melitz, 2015), thereby leading to even more U.S. imports from China. This theory predicts that industry clustering in China is positive for U.S. welfare because it reduces unit costs and thereby the terms of trade for the United States, but the reduction in workforce expertise and a loss of economies of scale in the U.S. are clear negatives in the long run.

Other, **non-economic arguments** for protectionism emphasise cultural aspects as an a reason for countries to protect certain industries from free trade and competition.

It is worth noting that protectionist arguments often emanate from workers, trade unions, and companies that are forced to compete with imports, with the strongest cries coming from those who may have lost their comparative advantage through improper management, inefficient operations or excessive labour rates.

3.1 Tariffs and Non-tariff Barriers

Trade barriers can be classified into two groups, tariffs and non-tariff barriers. Tariffs are relatively straightforward, involving a fee charged on imported goods. These either take the form of ad valorem tariffs based on the value of an import or what is known as a specific tariff that is charged for each specific unit. While tariffs are far more common, non-tariff barriers can take a number of forms.

Examples of non-tariff barriers

- Import quotas (e.g., 'voluntary export restraint' or 'orderly marketing agreements')
- Import licenses
- Import deposit schemes
- Import surcharges
- Rules of origin
- Anti-dumping measures
- Special labelling and packaging regulations
- Health and safety regulations
- Environmental regulations
- Customs procedures and documentation requirements
- Subsidies to domestic producers of import-competing goods
- Countervailing duties on subsidised imports
- Local content requirements
- Government contracts awarded only to domestic producers
- Exchange rate manipulation

Source: Global Shifts, Peter Dicken

As can be seen from the above list, even when high trade tariffs are largely absent from an economy, there may still be a number of 'beyond-tariff' issues which serve to dampen commerce. These often take the form of national standards or bureaucratic approval processes designed to make it burdensome for overseas companies to enter the domestic market in a meaningful way. So-called 'deep' trade agreements attempt to handle these issues. An example of soft trade barriers could be a Danish water conservation company trying to enter the Californian market with a new and innovative product. The product is approved in Denmark (and therefore in the single market in the EU) and sells to Danish institutions. Meanwhile, the market in California is considered to be attractive given the water scarcity there and the public's awareness of this challenge. Although there are no formal tariffs between the EU and United States for this particular product, some of the soft trade barriers, for example, are that Californian buyers are accustomed to Californian plumbing standards, and that product warranty legislation differs between the EU and United States.

If the EU and the US were to have a 'deep' trade agreement, issues like this would be addressed and trade between the two regions would be fully free. This would enable lower-cost access to the other's market and, because there would be only one product standard for this particular item, excess paperwork would be eliminated. This in turn would simplify product testing and certification, and economies of scale could be achieved.

It should be pointed out that not only do producers and consumers within a given free trade area benefit from the elimination of non-tariff barriers, but third-country producers also benefit from their removal since they can more easily sell their products within the given area. The creation of the single market in the EU offers an example of these benefits in practice.

Finally, it should be noted that the mere suggestion of possible tariff impositions – never mind the implementation itself – can lead to economic impacts. For example, investments in a given industry may fall if a tariff is threatened, or, conversely, investment may rise if tariffs are rumoured to be eliminated, whether through the WTO or by a government's unilateral decision.

3.2   Tariffs

Import tariffs are a classic example of a trade restriction imposed by one or more nations in order to hinder competition and imports from abroad. We start our analysis of import tariffs by examining a small nation which cannot influence global prices by its trade politics and is therefore is a price taker of imported products.

To develop our framework, we begin by looking at a *closed economy not trading* with other countries. We assume that the country's weekly demand for bicycles is expressed by the demand curve, D = €400 - €1Q. This curve reflects the fact that the consumer who is willing to pay the highest price pays €400 and that a new customer is added each time the price is lowered by €1.

Let us also assume that domestic supply is given by the supply curve, S = €100 + €1Q, where the minimum cost of €100 increases by €1 for each additional bicycle produced. If there is no international trade and the country produces all its bicycles domestically, the equilibrium point, where supply equals demand would be found at Price = €250 and Quantity = 150 bicycles. Put another way, at a price of €250 each, there will be a demand for 150 bicycles, which is exactly how many bicycles local producers will manufacture at that price. Finally, we assume that the country has full employment, i.e., that labour needed to produce bicycles beyond the equilibrium point must be taken from other productive sectors of the economy.

Figure 1. Supply and Demand in a Closed Economy

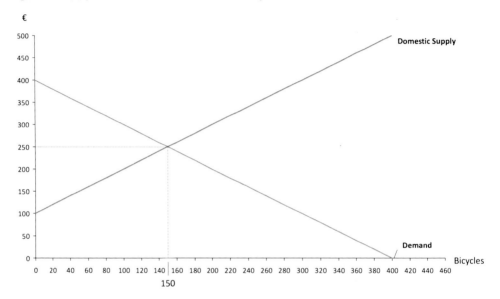

3.2.1 The Open Economy

When the country's economy is opened to free trade such that imports and exports are possible, we assume that the world price for bicycles is found to be Price = €150 because of comparative advantages in foreign countries. In other words, it is possible to import bicycles for €100 less than they sell for in the closed-economy case described above. This supply curve is horizontal because the country we are analysing is small and cannot influence global prices no matter how many bicycles they demand. Global production will always be much larger and is not impacted, as we illustrate below.

As can be seen, the demand for bicycles in the small country will now rise to 250 because of the lower price – up from the 150 bikes in a closed economy – and local production will decrease to 50 because of increased competition. Consumers will clearly win by receiving lower prices and an increased supply of bicycles. As a result, their consumers' surplus will increase as shown by the following equations:

150 x (€400-€250) x ½ = €11,250
to 250 x (€400-€150) x ½ = € 31,250

This equates to a total consumer surplus of € 20,000.

Figure 2. Domestic Supply, Global Supply and Demand in an Open Economy with Free Markets

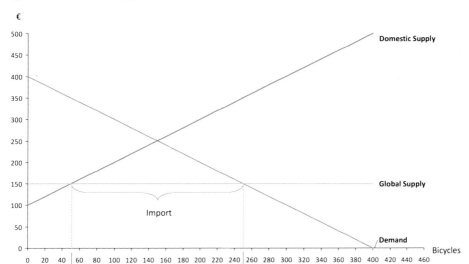

Concurrently, domestic producers will be required to scale down their level of production, and labour and capital will move from bicycle manufacturing to other comparatively more advantageous sectors of the economy. Producers' surplus in the domestic bicycle sector will therefore decrease as follows:

150 x (€250-€100) x ½ €11,250
to 50 x (€150-€100) x ½ €1,250,

This equates to a loss of €10,000 in producer surplus.

In summary, consumers will gain a surplus of €20,000, while domestic bicycle producers will lose a surplus of €10,000. This will lead to an overall surplus of 10,000. The country will import 200 bicycles from the global market and it will receive a net welfare benefit as a result of opening its doors to free trade.

3.2.2 Imposing an Import Tariff by a Small Country

Now suppose that local bicycle manufacturers convince the government to impose a €50 import tariff to protect the bicycle industry and its jobs from low-cost imports. Because this small country does not influence world prices the new global supply curve will equal the original free market supply curve horizontal at €150, plus the €50 levied as an import tariff. This is illustrated below where €50 is added to the Global Supply at the free market price of €150.

Figure 3. Economic Consequences of Imposing an Import Tariff by a Small Country

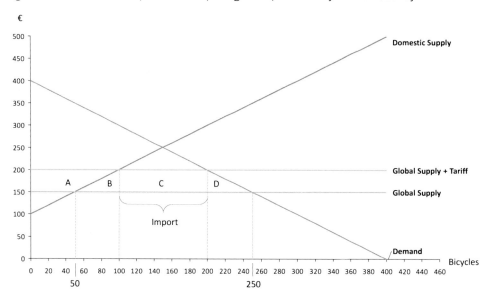

The country's terms of trade are not influenced by this policy change because net import prices are not impacted (i.e., global exporters will still sell bicycles at €150), but domestic consumers are charged the full amount of the tariff increase. As a result, they now face a higher price of €200 and will reduce their purchases accordingly to 200 bikes. In the end, consumers forfeit an amount of welfare equal to Area A+B+C+D becausee of the €50 price increase and the 50 fewer bicycles purchased. This equates to a welfare loss of 200 x €50 + 50 x €50 x ½= €11,250. There is a loss, firstly, because some consumers will now refrain from buying bicycles and, secondly, because those who continue buying must now pay a higher price than they paid under a free trade regime.

Local producers now receive a higher selling price and will increase their production from 50 bicycles to 100, thereby increasing their producers' surplus by ½× 50 × €50 + 50 × €50 = €3,750, which is equal to Area A. Imports will decrease from 200 to 100 bicycles and the government will levy a 100 × €50 = €5,000 import tariff, which is equal to Area C. For purposes of discussion we will assume this tariff is incorporated into the government budget and subsequently used for government spending.

The revenue effect is that the state receives more funds for government expenditures, but these are provided by consumers' tariff payments. Therefore, this is merely a wealth transfer from private citizens to the government, which is then returned to them via government spending. In other words, there is a redistribution of Area C from consumers to the government and then back to citizens. Naturally, this assumes that the government uses all of the import tariff revenue on productive, welfare-enhancing expenditures; if it does not, then part of the tariff revenue will be lost to unproductive transmission costs. Additionally, there will be administrative costs and other expenses associated with levying an import tariff which will also reduce the size of Area C.

At first glance, the increase in producer's surplus – Area A – can be considered a transfer of welfare from consumers to producers: consumers pay higher prices which benefit local producers, who in turn increase production. However, in 1967 the renowned economist Gordon Tullock pointed out that local producers have an interest in achieving and maintaining the protection inherent in an import tariff and are therefore willing to pay economic rent in the form of lobbying and other unproductive activities in order to achieve and maintain a situation which is in their subjective best interest. As long as the costs associated with maintaining this protection are lower than the potential increase in producers' surplus there is an incentive for them to continue paying this rent as long as politicians are also willing to undertake these negotiations on their behalf.

Area B is clearly a deadweight loss to society: local producers now produce bicycles at higher prices and higher costs than what they could have been produced for abroad. This represents an inefficient use of resources which fails to achieve an economic benefit. More capital, labour, and resources are allocated to the bicycle industry at increasing costs, simply because the domestic bicycle industry is being artificially protected due its lack of global competitiveness.

Area D is also a deadweight loss to society: it represents that portion of consumers and citizens in the domestic economy who do not buy bicycles at the higher price; they would have bought an imported bicycle at the free trade price, but not at the higher price which now prevails. Additionally, the consumers who are impacted by this welfare loss may be the less wealthy members of society who are no longer in a position to buy a bicycle.

In summary, national welfare has been reduced by Areas B and D, and significant welfare has been transferred from consumers to local producers in Area A and to the government in Area C. As bad as this is, national welfare will be reduced still further if this redistribution is inefficient, if it leads to local producers lobbying for continued protections, or if the government spends its tariff revenues on administrative costs and in unproductive, politically motivated ways.

3.2.3 Imposing an Import Tariff by a Large Country

For a larger country like the United States, or for the European Union as a whole, the analysis of the effect of import tariffs presented in the previous section could be different. This is because a large economy can influence global demand and prices simply by virtue of its size. Its import tariffs may lead foreign exporters to reduce their prices in order to maintain some of their market share in the large economy despite the imposition of tariffs. If they do, this improves the terms of trade for the larger country and gives it an economic advantage.

Figure 4. Supply and Demand in a Large, Closed Economy

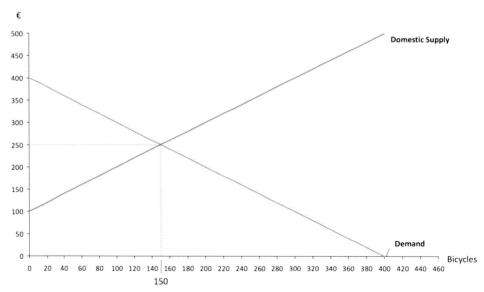

We will now analyse a similar situation to the previous example, only now we assume a large economy:

Because we are dealing with a large economy, domestic supply and demand are assumed to be per day. Otherwise the situation remains as it was before, with $S_D = €100 + €1Q$ and $D_D = €400 - €1Q$.

Assuming a closed economy with no trade, the price of a bicycle would be €250, with production of 150 units per day as illustrated above.

Global supply from the rest of the world can now be represented by $S_G = €100 + 0.25Q$. This reflects the fact that the country's economy is large enough such that if exports from abroad are reduced because of tariffs there will be pressure on foreign manufacturers to reduce their prices and offset a portion of the tariff in order to maintain exports to this country.

In an open economy with free trade, the total supply for a large economy would be the sum of domestic supply and global supply. This can be represented by the horizontal addition of the two supply functions:

$$S_D = 100 + Q \qquad => \quad Q = S_D - 100$$
$$S_G = 100 + 0{,}25Q \qquad => \quad Q = 4S_G - 400$$
$$\overline{\qquad\qquad Q = 5S_{D+G} - 500 \qquad => \quad S_{D+G} = 0.2Q + 100}$$

The total supply emanating from both domestic and global supply sources is therefore $S_{D+G} = 0.2Q + 100$.

Figure 5. Domestic Supply, Domestic + Global Supply and Demand in a Large Economy

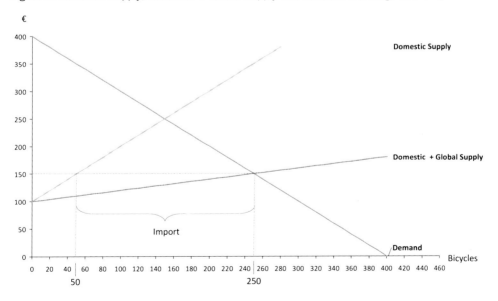

Equilibrium price will consequently decline to Price = €150, while equilibrium demand will rise to Q = 250 bicycles, with Q = 50 being produced domestically and Q = 200 being imported from abroad, as illustrated above:.

If a tariff of €50 is imposed, the analysis will be as follows:

The first 50 bicycles will be provided by domestic suppliers only since they are now protected by the €50 tariff. When the cost of bicycles in the large country has reached €150 at Q = 50, the €50 import tariff will be added to the global supply curve which will now be given by S_G = €150 + €0.25Q. Summing the global supply and domestic supply curves horizontally, we derive the following result:

$$S_D = 100 + Q \qquad => \quad Q = S_D - 100$$
$$\underline{S_G = 150 + 0{,}25Q \qquad => \quad Q = 4S_G - 600}$$
$$Q = 5S_{D+G} - 700 \qquad => \quad S_{D+G} = 0.2Q + 140$$

The total supply from domestic and global supply sources will thus be S_{D+G} = 0.2Q + 140.

If we now set this total supply curve equal to the domestic demand curve, we find that bicycles will increase in price from €150 to €183 after the tariff is imposed. This means that exporters will not pass on the entire €50 tariff to consumers but will absorb €17 of its burden, or 33 percent, by reducing their prices. These reductions will

Figure 6. Economic Consequences of Imposing an Import Tariff by a Large Economy

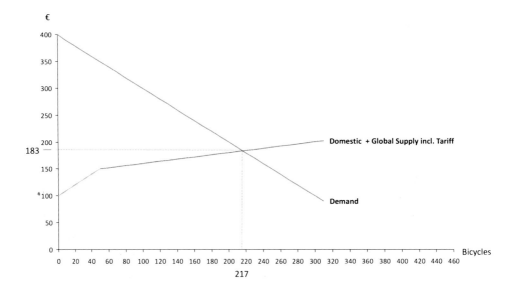

improve the large economy's terms of trade because net import prices have now been reduced. However, consumers will still see the price of bicycles increase from €150 to €183, however, and consumption will fall from 250 bicycles under free trade to 217 with the tariff. Domestic producers will increase production from 50 to 83 bicycles (€183 = €100 + €1Q => Q = 83) and increase their selling price to €183. This will cause imports to decline from 200 to 134.

We will now consider the tariff's impact on national welfare and income distribution.

Figure 7. Welfare Effects of Imposing an Import Tariff by a Large Economy

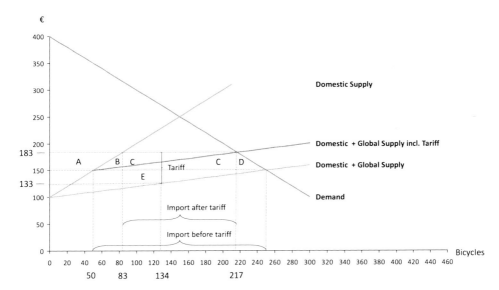

Overall, Area A+B+C+D represents reduced consumer surplus because consumers must now pay €183 instead of €150, meaning that some of them will no longer purchase bicycles.

Area A represents a redistribution of decreased consumer surplus to domestic producer surplus. Areas B and D are deadweight losses because of higher prices and lower volumes.

Area C+E equals the import tariff revenue received by the government since €50 per bicycle is paid on 134 imports. Area C equals the reduction in domestic consumer surplus as buyers must now pay €183 instead of €150 – i.e., consumers bear €33 of the import tariff. Compared to the case of the small nation where domestic consumers bear the entire cost of the €50 import tariff, here they bear only €33. This difference is unique to the large nation's case, because part of the tariff is borne by foreign exporters' lowering their prices. We can see this in Area E, which illustrates how foreign exporters reduce their export price by €17, from €150 to €133, in order stay competitive in the large country's market. Assuming that the large country's export prices remain unchanged, this reduction in import prices improves its terms of trade because the relative price of its exports to imports has improved because of the tariff. Thus, a large economy could potentially improve its terms of trade by levying an import tariff. However, this improvement comes at the cost of deadweight losses in Areas B and D, in addition to the transmission costs and economic rent associated with the government and producers benefitting from higher bicycle prices as consumers are forced to pay more.

It must be noted that the large country's strategy to improve its terms of trade through the imposition of tariffs is not without its caveats. Most importantly, one nation's imposing import tariffs may well result in retaliation by its trading partners. The end result is a loss of goodwill and a tit-for-tat, beggar-thy-neighbour policy which will likely lead to a decrease in welfare for all of countries involved. Ultimately countries find themselves in a classic prisoner's dilemma where the total outcome could be improved if everyone cooperated with one another, but where the risk is that each country tries to optimise its own outcome by hindering its trading partners.

Other examples of beggar-thy-neighbour trading policies include a country's keeping its currency artificially low in order to boost exports or establishing import quotas to help domestic companies gain a competitive advantage against foreigners. If other countries follow suit, as they are often tempted to, all parties will lose out on economic gains.

In the long run, as well, protectionist trade policies hold negative consequences for a country. The reasoning is as follows: assuming that a country's domestic savings and investments remain unchanged by protectionist measures, its net exports will also be static since macroeconomic equilibrium is reached when net savings equals net exports.[1] How is this negative for a country? First, trade restrictions will reduce the quantity of imports. Assuming that exports are initially unaffected by the imposition of trade restrictions, a reduction in imports means that net exports (exports minus imports) must rise. However, domestic producers who compete against imports will now benefit from these restrictive trade policies and subsequently raise their prices. This will increase the price of domestic goods vs. imported goods, thereby diminishing their competitiveness on the international markets and leading to a

---

1. In macroeconomic terms, $S - I = NX$ in the long run

devalued currency since there will now be less foreign demand for the nation's goods. This currency devaluation may, in turn, lead to inflation back home or to a decline in the terms of trade, either of which will lead to reduced exports. The net effect of imposing tariffs, then, will be a reduction in both the country's exports and imports. It would then experience less overall trade and consequently higher prices. It would also suffer from a lower variety of products in the country, and reduced specialisation as it would now need to begin producing goods in which it has no distinct comparative advantage.

The increase in price of imported goods may also impact export-oriented companies since they often use imported goods as inputs in their own production. This is particularly true if the import tariffs are placed on raw materials like steel or aluminum which are used in countless industrial applications, or on goods which are employed as inputs for further value-added processes. Due to the higher prices which domestic manufacturers must charge as a result of import tariffs, they may lose international competitiveness as an unintended consequence of their government's decision.

Another economic consequence could be that the higher price of imported goods increases the cost of living in the country. This in turn could motivate workers to demand higher wages, in a case of so-called imported inflation. Additionally, as new firms enter industries which were previously dominated by imports, these import substitution efforts could increase the demand for labour which would cause production costs to rise. This would only serve to further weaken the country's competitiveness on the international markets.

As we close this chapter, a final point to be considered is that in a globalised world it is not always clear where goods and services are actually produced. In Chapter 1 we saw that global value chains can shift production to the most economically beneficial location, when needed. With the free flow of capital, it is therefore possible that corporations could move production to a different geographical jurisdiction in order to avoid tariffs and the negative impacts they impose. Countries therefore need to be careful what they wish when they seek to restrict free trade: unintended consequences are almost certain to ensue, especially in a globalised world.

CHAPTER 4

Financial Globalisation in Recent Decades

In the waning decades of the 20th century the rise of globalisation discussed in Chapter 1 took the financial markets by storm. According to McKinsey Global Institute;

'Between 1990 and 2000, the stock of foreign investment liabilities relative to GDP more than doubled, from 42 percent of world GDP to 96 percent. Between 2000 and the financial market peak of 2007, the figure nearly doubled again to reach 185 percent.'

The New Dynamics of Financial Globalization, 2017, p. 37

In the decade since the stock market's top and the start of the global financial crisis, the level of foreign investment relative to GDP has remained high and in 2016 stood at an estimated 183 percent.

In this chapter we will study global financial flows, first based on the classical macroeconomic understanding that excess savings in surplus countries creates global capital flows which serve to finance deficit countries. Sometimes referred to as the 'Excess Savings' view, this perspective is focused on **net capital flows.** We then examine this classical view in light of the massive global capital flows seen today, given that they derive not only from commerce in the **real economy** as suggested by the classical view, but also, and perhaps even more importantly, from capital flows connected to **financial asset trading.** This means that financial flows are connected to both **net and gross capital flows**, which has implications for the world economy, as we shall see.

4.1 Net Capital Flows

We start our discussion by analysing the link between trade and financial flows, which is reflected in a country's **balance of payments**.

The term 'balance of payments' summarises the net result of inflows vs. outflows of foreign currency to a country. It consists of the following elements:

Foreign currency inflows:

- Export of goods and services
- Factor payments and transfers from abroad
- Capital transfers from abroad
- Financial assets sold abroad
- Direct foreign investments into home country
- Decrease in foreign currency reserves

Foreign currency outflows:

- Imported goods and services
- Factor payments and transfers to foreign countries
- Capital transfers to foreign countries
- Acquisition of financial assets abroad
- Direct foreign investments made abroad
- Increase in foreign currency reserves

The sum of exports minus imports gives net exports, also known as the **trade balance**. Adding factor payments to this sum gives the current account. If a country's current account is negative there will be a savings deficit which must then be financed on a net basis via funds from abroad. Consequently, a country's total savings deficit and the current account must be equal to one another. Thus, the current account is the sum of net savings from both the public and the private sectors of an economy:

$$\text{Current account} = (G - T) + (I - S)$$

Where: G is government spending
　　　 T is tax revenue
　　　 I is private investments, and
　　　 S is private savings

According to this classical Excess Savings view, the global flow of funds to finance capital accumulation and the international flow of goods and services mirror one another. Equilibrium is established through the financial account, which consists of the net value of financial assets and foreign direct investments acquired or sold. The stock of foreign reserves is managed by a country's central bank and utilised to control the exchange rate if needed.

A country with a trade surplus will export more than it imports. This will lead to an accumulation of excess funds which can be used either to reduce foreign liabilities or increase financial assets abroad. As a result, the country will have net capital outflows equal to its trade surplus. This surplus will allow it to finance countries with trade deficits, which means that macroeconomic savings in one country can serve as the source of loans to deficit countries. This perspective tightly links global capital flows to trade flows. As such, it leads to a build-up of foreign currency reserves for surplus countries which offers a close reflection of their trade balance and current account. On the global financial markets this surplus or deficit is equal to the supply and demand for a given country's currency, so trade deficits, for example, tend to put downward pressure on a country's currency.

Another way of understanding the relationship between a country's net exports, current account, and currency exchange rate is to consider things from the perspective of foreign investors: when foreigners buy U.S. assets such as land, real assets, and company stocks, they do not do it to finance the U.S. current account deficit but rather because they consider U.S. assets to be an attractive investment relative to other opportunities elsewhere in the world. When they transfer funds into the United States to buy these assets, it creates an inbound capital flow in the form of money which foreigners have earned abroad selling their goods and services. Capital inflows increase the demand for dollars, which causes the dollar to appreciate against other currencies. A stronger dollar reduces U.S. exports since people overseas can buy less of a given U.S. product for the same amount of local currency. On the other hand, it increases U.S. imports because the dollar will buy more of the same foreign good than it could before, which naturally spurs demand. As exports decrease and imports rise, the United States will consequently experience a current account deficit over time. In practice this is exactly what has occurred. Since the 1980s the U.S. has run a deficit in its current account which now equates to more than $450 billion per year (cf. Figure 1, Chapter 2).

Theoretically, the sum of global current account deficits should equal the sum of global current account surpluses because a decrease in one nation's deficit can only take place if another country sees its overall surplus decline. Stated another way, the world will see net exports (total exports minus total imports) diminish if the global current account deficit declines.

This classical view, however, is modified by the impact of financial globalisation. In particular, with financial globalisation comes access to a larger and deeper pool of savings which is able to finance current account deficits, thereby allowing them to expand beyond what traditional macroeconomic theory would predict. This is especially true for countries regarded as safe havens – i.e., places where capital can be safely invested due to their level of market stability and historically attractive returns, or, in the case of the United States, because it holds the reserve currency of the world.

The Role of the Dollar in the International Economy

A reserve currency is a national currency which is used as a medium of exchange, unit of account, and store of value across the globe. It is therefore held in large amounts by governments, central banks, and corporations for use in international transactions. When a common currency is used by importers and exporters to quote prices and kept in reserve by central banks, financial intermediaries are able to bypass the conversion costs of currency exchange and thus increase the liquidity of their assets. Thanks to the dollar's reserve currency status, the United States Government and its citizens are able to borrow money from abroad and purchase imports for a slightly lower financing cost and without exchange rate risk, an advantage termed 'exorbitant privilege'.

When people and businesses trade in dollars because most others also do as well, they are said to enjoy the 'network externalities' of widespread use. Furthermore, the dollar's long-term stability, due in part to the Fed maintaining low inflation for over three decades, makes it an attractive investment option for savers in countries with higher inflation. Most importantly, the market for U.S. Treasury bonds is the largest, safest, and most liquid financial market in the world.

After the 2008 global financial crisis, China created swap lines to supply renminbi to 15 foreign central banks, including those of Australia and Singapore. As a result, China's use of the renminbi in international trade has grown from around 3 percent in 2008 to an estimated 33 percent today. In a major step of international recognition, in September 2016 the IMF included the renminbi for the first time in its reserve asset basket of elite currencies known as Special Drawing Rights (SDRs), thereby joining the dollar, euro, yen, and pound sterling.

The New Dynamics of Financial Globalization, 2017

The following table shows that as of 2017, U.S. dollars still make up the majority of official foreign exchange reserves with a 62.7 percent share, but that the rate is gradually decreasing. At roughly 20 percent, the euro is its only potential competitor at present, though China, for instance, bears watching; its renminbi entered the scene in 2016 and despite comprising only 1.23 percent of official reserves it may be poised to increase.

We have seen how extended periods of current account deficits (negative savings) leads to increasing net foreign debt. Whether or not a country's running deficits in perpetuity and accumulating large-scale foreign debts is a problem in today's liberalised and financially globalised world constitutes an important and ongoing discussion. One key condition for the situation to continue involves all parties having access to

Table 1. World Currency Composition of Official Foreign Exchange Reserves

	2014	2015	2016	2017
Shares of Allocated Reserves	58,68	67,91	78,59	87,69
Shares of U.S. dollars	65,14	65,72	65,34	62,70
Shares of euros	21,20	19,14	19,13	20,15
Shares of Chinese renminbi			1,08	1,23
Shares of Japanese yen	3,54	3,75	3,95	4,89
Shares of pounds sterling	3,70	4,71	4,34	4,54
Shares of Australian dollars	1,59	1,77	1,69	1,80
Shares of Canadian dollars	1,75	1,77	1,94	2,02
Shares of Swiss francs	0,24	0,27	0,16	0,18
Shares of other currencies	2,83	2,86	2,37	2,50
Shares of Unallocated Reserves	41,32	32,09	21,41	12,31

Source: IMF Currency Composition of Official Foreign Exchange Reserves (COFER)

perfect information. As long as this exists net foreign debt would not be a problem in principle since agents in surplus countries would gladly finance the needs of deficit countries. The other condition is that the debtor nation's savings deficit not be driven by excessive consumption or exorbitant fiscal deficits. Rather, it should ideally stem from investments in productive capital which will increase the country's future economic output so that it can service its debt over time. Norway offers an illustrative example. In the 1960s it needed to import a massive amount of technology and knowledge when it discovered oil and gas in the North Sea. These investments and the consequent current account deficits were financed by borrowing from foreign investors who regarded this as an attractive opportunity to enjoy attractive returns on productive capital. This indeed proved to be the case as the North Sea oilfields led to Norway's becoming one of the largest oil and gas exporters in the world, with substantial current account surpluses and enormous investments abroad. Nonetheless, even if it were deemed acceptable (though not optimal) to run current account deficits for extended periods of time, it is important to understand whether a country's capital inflows consist of long-term foreign direct investment or short-term portfolio allocations which are chasing a higher return. As we will see later in this chapter when we discuss gross capital flows, this distinction can have significant ramifications for a country's exchange rate.

Global capital flows, especially those of eurocurrencies,[1] grew substantially during the 1960s to 1990s as capital markets were liberalised and access to overseas investment opportunities became easier with the rise of information technology.

The main beneficiary of these global capital flows was Asia, so much so that through 1999 it attracted nearly half of all FDI destined for the developing world. The allure of Asia was that it was undergoing the fastest industrialisation in the history of the world thanks the landmark economic reforms instituted in 1978 by Chinese premier, Deng Xiaoping, in 1978, and as a result of the greater regional stability enjoyed after the end of the Vietnam war. This growth required capital - lots of it - and to attract it Asia paid top dollar Interest rates, with the result that massive amounts of capital flowed in from around the world.

These capital flows to Asia and elsewhere were made possible because during the 1990s, the *capital controls* on cross border flows which had been implemented in the aftermath of the Great Depression finally began to ease or were removed altogether in many cases. This in turn allowed *exchange rates* to float more freely, thus dramatically changing two of the three components of the so-called trilemma or impossibility triangle – the third being *independent monetary policy*. As outlined in Chapter 1, the general rule is that a country can only control two of these three at a time. These changes, as much as anything, helped spur the rise of financial globalisation.

USC and UCLA economics researchers Joshua Aizenman and Rodrigo Pinto (2013: 639), however, point out that the three elements of the trilemma are not mutually exclusive in reality; rather, it is a question of the *levels* of free capital flows, the *levels* of exchange rate volatility, and the *levels* of monetary independence which a nation employs. They document that,

'while developing countries have been hovering around intermediary levels of monetary independence and slightly deviating from the cross-country average, industrialized countries have steadily become much less independent in terms of monetary policy, reflecting decisions made by the euro member countries. With the introduction of the euro in 1999, Euro-zone countries drastically increased the level of exchange rate stability while developing countries continued to remain around the mid-level of exchange rate flexibility. Not surprisingly, industrialized countries have achieved higher levels of financial openness with emerging market countries sharply increasing their financial openness after 1990 while settling for moderate level of exchange rate flexibility and monetary policy independence.'

---

1. Eurocurrencies are currencies deposited outside the currency's home country. They can, for example, be dollars held in a European bank, or euros held in a Brazilian bank. The term is not constricted to only euro, but all currencies held outside of the home country of that currency.

As global capital markets became increasingly liberalised during the 1990s, emerging markets – especially those of Asia – built up substantial reserves of hard currency. One perspective on this development argues that large cash reserves were accumulated in order to ensure that these countries' central banks could control or manage exchange rates in a world where financial markets were fully globalised. This way, if capital suddenly fled the country as portfolio investments or 'hot money' rushed for the exits, threatening to devalue the local currency due to an unexpected immediate demand for dollars, the central banks would still have enough resources to inject the necessary dollars into the economy and stabilise the local currency.

According to Aizenman and Pinto (2013: 636),

'Bretton Woods viewed financial integration and global imbalances as a win-win configuration – the allegedly superior financial intermediation of the USA absorbed the excess savings of the rapidly growing countries, facilitating their growth as the USA became the demander of last resort. The massive accumulation of international reserves was seen as the counterpart of the Bretton Woods system, whereby the USA benefited from the 'exorbitant privilege' of funding its fiscal and current account deficits in U.S. dollars at a lower cost, while China enjoyed export led growth.'

The importance of emerging markets having enough foreign currency reserves to serve as a buffer against the external shocks of globalisation hit home in an unforgettable way for Asia in 1997. From the late 1980s to mid-1990s Thailand, Indonesia, and South Korea in particular ran large current account deficits but maintained fixed exchange rate pegs to the dollar. This encouraged enormous borrowing in dollar-denominated debt which fuelled the so-called 'East Asian Economic Miracle'. For a number of years these countries enjoyed rapid industrialisation, export-oriented policies, lower income inequality, and an average seven percent annual economic growth. It was boom times for the so-called Asian Tigers.

Then in the mid-1990s the U.S. Federal Reserve increased interest rates to head off inflation as the U.S. economy recovered from recession. Increased rates made dollars more attractive and caused the U.S. currency to rise. A higher dollar then pressured the East Asian economies' export-oriented growth as their products became more expensive on the world markets. As exports slowed the Tiger's growth model became tenuous and a widespread economic downturn ensued. As it gathered force, international lenders who had invested hundreds of billions of dollars in this region began to worry about over-exposure and the ability of the region's creditors to repay their non-performing loans. The financial globalisation equivalent of a 'run on the bank' ensued as lenders withdrew credit, thereby creating a credit crunch with their unwillingness to lend. Investors became worried and a stampede of hot money began to rush for the exits.

The crisis reached a cresendo in July 1997 as Thailand's currency was hit with a massive speculative attack designed to test whether its dollar peg could hold. The Thai government was determined to keep the peg place but ran out of currency reserves too soon. When it was finally forced to let the Thai baht float freely on the open market to relieve the built-up pressure of the peg's insatiable demand for dollars, its currency entered free fall and quickly lost more than half its value. Unable to pay their dollar-denominated debts any longer, corporations and institutions declared bankruptcy which in turn brought Thailand's soaring economy to a screeching halt. Unemployment spiked, inflation ran wild as more and more baht were printed amidst the devaluation, and the stock market plunged by 75%. Panic spread to the other Asian Tigers and fears of contagion gripped the globe. Finally, the IMF stepped in with a $20 billion loan so that Thailand could stanch the bleeding. In exchange it demanded that new bankruptcy laws be put in place and that much stricter regulations be adopted by banks and other financial institutions who had engaged in unwise lending. It took four years for the Thai economy to recover (until 2001), and another two for it to repay its debt to the World Bank, but the lessons of the dangers of hot money have remained.

Ultimately the entire Asian region was affected by this crisis and suffered a temporary slump in consumer demand for exports and a hit to its reputation as an economic powerhouse. However, this economic shock treatment motivated many Asian countries to secure their financial stability by building up large foreign exchange reserves through mercantilist approaches which emphasised large trade surpluses and maintaining their currencies at low values.

By building up significant international reserves, they were, by and large, able to weather the 2008 global financial crisis in relatively good condition. Their hard currency reserves reduced sovereign risk premia, which deterred speculative currency attacks. As mentioned above, Aizenmann and Pinto argue that many emerging markets chose a middle-ground approach to financial deregulation and the impossibility triangle/trilemma, whereas many OECD countries deregulated too much which consequently pushed financial globalisation too far.

Ultimately this period seems to have been characterised by volatile financial flows and currency fluctuations, as well as a tendency for regions to handle their challenges internally, especially in the case of Europe and Asia.

The Excessive Savings view would thus argue that the build-up of imbalances led to an accumulation of foreign reserves, while lower interest rates fuelled a private credit boom in the developed world. China and Japan especially invested large amounts of foreign currency reserves in U.S. securities, thereby contributing to enormous net capital outflows from Asia, which helped to push down long-term interest rates in the United States. Cheap credit, in turn, drove a consumption boom and housing bubble across America as many people used their credit cards to the limit and bought houses well beyond their means. Before 2007, this growth in consumption and private spending drew more imports from abroad, which added to the trade surplus of Asian economies and led to more excess savings that was recycled in the form of exports to West. The imbalances became unsustainable in 2007, and soon after this the 2008 Great Financial Crisis struck. Though the global imbalances began to ease, as massive fiscal deficit spending in the U.S. and Europe drove a meagre economic recovery, these over-spending patterns soon began to re-emerge.

In 1960, the Belgian economist Robert Triffin warned the U.S. Congress that the fast-growing global market's demand for dollars would put continued pressure on its economy to run current account deficits, with the alternative being a crisis of inadequate international liquidity. As it happened, almost fifty years later the United Nations Conference on Trade and Development (UNCTAD) issued a 2009 report on the causes of the global financial crisis the year before. The reason they identified? The dollar's dominance had led to build-up of U.S. current account deficits and emerging market savings surpluses which precipitated the global financial crisis of 2008. Triffin had been prescient. Contrary to the popular saying, deficits do matter.

Another possible source of global imbalance today is the deregulation of the financial system. After the Great Depression's strict regulations designed to limit risk-taking by banks and financial institutions, a wave of deregulation began in the late-1980s which allowed banks to become active investors. As the financial sectors of the United States and Europe rapidly expanded, there was a de-linking of the institutions issuing loans from those eventually holding them on their balance sheets. This growth in bank lending was concentrated in residential mortgages in mature economies, with four main types of risk-takers playing a central role in the onset of the 2008 financial crisis: government-supported entities, investment banks, hedge funds, and off-balance sheet vehicles.

How about today, a full decade later? Where does the global financial system stand? Prior to the crisis, the net financial and capital account imbalances had grown sharply, peaking in 2007 at 2.6 percent of global GDP, or $1.3 trillion. Since the crisis, the imbalances have slowed moderately to a still significant 1.7 percent of global GDP or $1.5 trillion (*The New Dynamics of Financial Globalization*, 2017, p. 56).

Though we have rightly focused on net capital flows in the real economy throughout this section, the continued financialization of the global economy seems to point to gross capital flows playing an increasingly central role in today's globalised economy. It is to this topic that we now turn our attention.

4.2   Gross Capital Flows

Challenging the classical view of excess savings being the determining factor for global capital flows, Borio and Disyatat (BIS, 2011: 1) argue that,

'By construction, current accounts and net capital flows reveal little about financing. They capture changes in net claims on a country arising from trade in real goods and services and hence net resource flow. But they exclude the underlying changes in gross flows and their contributions to existing stocks, including all the transactions involving only trade in financial assets, which make up the bulk of cross-border financial activity. The misleading focus on current accounts arguably reflects the failure to distinguish sufficiently clearly between saving and financing. Saving, as defined in the national accounts, is simply income (output) not consumed, financing, a cash flow concept, is access to purchasing power in the form of an accepted settlement medium (money), including through borrowing. Investment, and expenditures more generally, require financing, not saving.'

A key point here is the distinction between gross capital flows and net capital flows. **Net capital flows** only reflect the net effect of all capital inflows minus all capital outflows. As described in the previous section, it is therefore equal to the current account – that is, to trade in *real* goods and services. **Gross capital flows**, however, measure the total annual foreign capital inflows and outflows, regardless of any direct link to trade. As a result, the buying and selling of financial assets and liabilities in today's global financial system creates gross capital flows which are substantially greater than net capital flows and have no direct bearing on trade or current accounts. They are purely monetary in nature and can be quite volatile, since, unlike traded goods and services, they can cross borders with little effort and negligible cost.

Borio and Disyatat (2011) show how gross capital flows rose from about 10 percent of global GDP in 1998 to over 30 percent in 2007, just prior to the Great Financial Crisis. By far, the most significant capital flows took place between the United States and Europe, and since Europe's current account is nearly balanced this fact does not correlate well with the Excess Savings view that surplus countries finance deficit countries – in this case the United States. According to McKinsey Global Institute,

'Gross capital flows – particularly cross-border lending – remain volatile. Since 2010, in any given year one-third of developing and two-thirds of advanced economies experience a large decline or surge in total capital flows. The median change is equivalent to 6.7 % of GDP for developing countries and 10.8 % for advanced countries. These fluctuations create large swings in exchange rates and could reduce macroeconomic stability. Cross-border lending is particularly volatile. Over the past five years, more than 60 percent of developing countries and over 70 percent of advanced economies experienced a large decline, surge, reversal, or recovery in cross-border lending each year, making volatility the norm rather than the exception.'

The New Dynamics of Financial Globalization, 2017, p. 11

Back in 2001, Argentina defaulted on its foreign debt obligations and was barred from accessing the international bond markets until 2016. In April 2016, as the lock-out period finally expired, the country floated a $16.5 billion sovereign bond. From that point forward Argentina's dollar-denominated debt has steadily increased, leading to continued concerns by investors. In May 2018, the Argentine central bank was forced to increase domestic interest rates to above 30 percent due to rapid depreciation of the Argentine peso despite the fact that earlier in the year, the central bank had sold significant amounts of U.S. dollars in a bid to support the currency. The fact that a runaway devaluation nonetheless occurred is partly explained by capital flowing out of Argentina due to anticipated interest rate increases by the U.S. Federal Reserve.

According to the Institute of International Finance, 'Since mid-April 2018, $5.6 billion has flowed out of emerging market debt and securities. The rise in U.S. bond yields along with a stronger dollar are prompting a downturn in portfolio flows to emerging markets'.

Putting it all together, this situation illustrates how developing economies with a high dollar-denominated debt burden are vulnerable to gross global capital flows as hot money continually seeks a greater rate of return.

Bordo et al. (2000) show that the number of financial crises since 1973 has doubled compared to the 1945-1973 period and that banking crises, too, have become increasingly more frequent. Both of these are signs that the gradual transition of the global economy over the post-Bretton Woods period has been one of real capital economy to a financially-driven one. One significant contributor to this transition was the deregulation of the U.S. financial sector begun during the 1980s and greatly increased by the 1999 repeal of the Depression-era Glass-Steagall Act. This legislation had prevented commercial banks from engaging in investment banking activities, but its removal helped fuel the financial globalisation of today as new types of exotic financial instruments were devised. These derivatives allowed investment banks to do many previously unheard-of things, such as for instance, to securitise real estate mortgages.

According to Harvard economist Dani Rodrik, these short-term capital flows, *are hardly a sideshow or a minor blemish in international capital flows; they are the main story'*. Furthermore, according to Jonathan Ostry, Deputy Director of Economic Research at the IMF (2006), short-term portfolio cash flows seem to lead to boom-and-bust volatility and, in some cases, financial crises.

Another element of global finance which has gained the ascendancy in recent decades involves so-called shadow banks – financial institutions that, like traditional banks, are at the centre of financial intermediation but which, unlike them, do not engage in traditional corporate or individual lending and are not subject to the same regulatory oversight as traditional deposit-taking banks. Examples include hedge funds, pension funds, insurance companies, private equity firms, and investment banks such as Bear Sterns and Lehman Brothers whose ill-starred, hot-money driven forays into sub-prime mortgage lending lit the fuse to the 2008 global financial crisis.

Princeton economist Robert Gilpin has stated that, '*As international finance has more tightly integrated national markets, states have responded by increasing the level of trade protectionism.*' (Gilpin 1987). In a similar vein, the famed economist and titan of industry, Rimmer Devries, observed in 1990 that, '*There is a certain tension in maintaining both free capital and free trade. The difficulty of repressing capital flows makes for a tendency to compensate ill effects by giving ground on free trade*' (De Vries, 1990). These observations indicate a potential conflict in having both free trade and free capital flows take place simultaneously – a consideration which also lay behind the Bretton Woods and the IMF thinking that floating exchange rates would create instability and have a deleterious impact on international trade.

4.3   Recent Trends in Financial Globalisation

Despite the contraction in global finance since the global financial crisis, the McKinsey Global Institute calculates that the value of foreign investment as share of global GDP is little changed since 2007, down from 185 percent of GDP in 2007 to 183 percent in 2016 (*The New Dynamics of Financial Globalization, 2017*). Consequently, global financial markets continue to be highly interconnected. One key difference since the turn of the 21st century, though, is the composition of these foreign investments: the percentage of equities held by foreigners increased from 17 percent to 27 percent, while bonds rose from 18 percent to 31 percent. Seen from another perspective, FDI and equity flows increased to make up 69 percent of cross-border capital flows in 2016, up from 36 percent prior to 2007.

Consequently, lending and other investments have declined during the same period. Global finance thus seems to have moved in the direction of longer-term investments, which may reduce the risk of short-term capital movements and related volatility.

McKinsey Global Institute (MGI) publishes an annual Financial Connectedness Ranking of 100 countries which measures their total stock of foreign investment assets and liabilities. The data are interesting in that they reveal a number of insights about the stocks of foreign assets, their interrelatedness, and the fact that although advanced economies top the list, emerging markets are increasing their share significantly, especially China, Indonesia, and Brazil.

The observation that in the post-financial crisis years various developing countries (other than China) are becoming net recipients of global capital rather than net providers, is a sea change from the recent past, according to McKinsey Global Institute. Classical economic theory predicts that diminishing returns on capital will prompt investors from rich countries to seek the higher returns available in poorer countries with lower stocks of capital. Stated another way, net capital flows should

Table 2. MGI Financial Connectedness Ranking, 2016

Country	Total in USD Billion		Foreign Assets % of GDP					Foreign Liabilities % of GDP				Foreign Assets and Liabilities/ GDP
	Foreign Assets	Foreign Liabilities	FDI	Equity	Debt securities	Loans and others	Foreign reserves	FDI	Equity	Debt securities	Loans and others	
United States	21.708	29.922	40	38	15	21	2	39	35	59	28	278
Luxembourg	10.643	10.825	9088	3016	3460	2332	2	8231	6376	1797	1799	36101
United Kingdom	10.577	10.492	71	64	71	191	5	59	58	99	183	801
Netherlands	8.045	7.970	659	109	116	155	5	578	86	206	167	2077
Germany	8.064	6.617	57	29	57	84	5	42	20	61	68	424
Japan	8.215	5.472	29	29	50	35	25	5	30	28	48	277
France	6.149	6.983	66	30	72	76	6	44	35	109	96	533
China	6.594	4.739	12	2	1	15	29	26	5	2	9	101
Ireland	4.963	5.572	478	331	511	370	1	474	903	183	338	3588
Hong Kong, China	4.471	3.402	537	274	153	310	120	574	135	16	336	2455
Switzerland	4.290	3.537	232	93	98	125	103	192	145	16	183	1186
Canada	3.212	3.071	83	66	19	36	5	66	30	65	39	411
Italy	2.713	2.878	34	43	33	28	9	26	10	66	53	302
Singapore	2.976	2.350	230	174	171	344	83	359	52	13	368	1793
Spain	1.760	2.906	55	20	25	38	5	60	25	69	81	378
Belgium	2.142	2.012	197	67	76	114	5	213	27	97	94	890
Australia	1.471	2.277	35	32	18	27	4	51	30	69	31	298
Sweden	1.414	1.448	94	81	25	65	12	81	49	95	58	560
Norway	1.529	796	58	172	114	53	16	52	23	71	69	628
Brazil	772	1.486	17	1	<1	4	20	43	14	13	13	126
Russia	1.226	926	33	<1	5	28	29	32	11	4	25	168
South Korea	1.218	928	22	13	9	17	26	13	27	13	12	152
Austria	909	967	82	28	52	68	6	74	15	98	64	485
Denmark	930	793	77	78	60	68	21	51	60	86	61	562
Mexico	582	1.065	14	0	5	19	17	45	12	31	14	157
India	540	933	6	<1	<1	2	16	14	7	4	17	65
Finland	638	707	65	73	64	63	4	51	52	91	104	568
Saudi Arabia	930	304	13	17	12	20	84	36	3	<1	8	193
Indonesia	296	669	8	<1	1	10	12	30	11	14	16	103
Portugal	352	556	41	17	46	55	12	72	15	47	138	443
South Africa	409	414	59	48	3	13	16	48	50	24	19	280
Thailand	379	433	23	4	5	18	42	51	25	9	22	200
Poland	242	548	14	4	2	8	24	51	8	26	33	169
Turkey	215	571	4	<1	<1	8	12	16	4	13	34	92
Greece	247	517	15	6	61	41	4	16	6	18	226	393
Mauritius	379	357	1687	992	92	362	40	2142	195	71	577	6158
Malaysia	387	348	51	16	8	23	33	44	18	27	28	248
Chile	329	379	48	41	19	10	16	99	10	24	20	287
Israel	382	275	32	19	18	20	31	35	26	9	16	206
Hungary	267	355	159	5	3	25	21	203	10	32	37	496
Argentina	278	221	7	<1	<1	40	4	16	2	8	14	91
Czech Republic	208	264	22	7	8	26	44	77	3	25	33	244
Venezuela	251	116	11	<1	1	71	5	10	<1	6	25	128
Philippines	162	193	15	<1	4	7	26	22	16	9	17	117
Nigeria	131	182	3	6	1	16	6	23	<1	10	11	77
Peru	104	180	1	14	2	5	31	50	5	17	20	146
Morocco	38	107	5	2	<1	6	24	54	3	8	39	140

go from rich countries to poorer ones. However, the opposite has often proven to be the case – developing countries have provided more capital to the global system than they have received. This trend was dubbed the Lucas Paradox, colloquially known as 'capital flowing uphill'. Proposed by renowned University of Chicago economist Robert Lucas, this paradox explains how higher sovereign risk, asymmetric information, and incomplete markets all limit the appetite of global investors for projects in developing countries, while also reducing their ability to absorb inbound FDI effectively. For many years, developing countries such as China, and major oil producers such as Algeria, Iraq, Mexico, and Saudi Arabia, had large export surpluses, leaving them with an abundance of foreign capital. Central banks in these countries invested their surpluses in safe, liquid global assets such as foreign currencies, U.S. Treasuries, and other bonds. In recent years, however, with lower commodity prices and a smaller trade surplus in China, the capital outflows from export-oriented central banks have dwindled and the trend has reversed (*The New Dynamics of Financial Globalisation, 2017*). Nevertheless, from 2005 to 2016, the stock of Chinese FDI assets rose from USD 64 billion to USD 1.38 trillion, with roughly 55 percent of this investment in advanced economies and 45 percent directed to the developing world.

The Political Economy of De-Globalizing Processes

By Associate Professor, Edward Ashbee, Chair and Programme Director: BSc/MSc International Business and Politics, Copenhagen Business School

This chapter considers processes of political and economic de-globalization. The term was popularized by Walden Bello who put it forward in 2002 as a progressive rallying cry to those who, like him, sought the capture of economic power by nations, communities and localities. Bello championed alternatives to multinational operations and global neoliberalism so that production can '... take place at the community and national level ...' (Bello, 2002: 114).

Nonetheless, while Bello put forward de-globalization as a way forward for the left and a challenge to multinational capital, the term was employed very differently, but much more widely, in the wake of the 2008 to 2009 financial crisis. In its later incarnation, 'de-globalization' was used by those closer to the political mainstream and tied to their profound anxieties about the future of the global order. Although Bello put forward de-globalization in normative terms and called for de-globalizing initiatives, it was subsequently framed as a positive statement (and thus purported to be objective) albeit one with heavily normative overtones. Drawing upon events and developments in the US and Europe, most notably Brexit, the concept was understood as a claim that processes of globalization had been thrown into reverse. This, it was said, would almost certainly impede economic growth and foster reactionary nationalisms.

Concepts

The term 'de-globalization' is of course a twist upon the word 'globalization', a term that has been in circulation for many decades. Globalization had suggested that processes of production, distribution and exchange now stretched across borders and continents and national markets were thereby being integrated with each other. Capital, goods and, most visibly, labour were moving much more freely. As the global economy shifted towards digital exchanges, services and knowledge, the traditional barriers imposed by distance and oceans mattered much less. 'Hot money' was travelling across the world in a relentless search for the highest rate of return. The world economy was furthermore subject to a degree of governance by global institutions including the World Trade Organization, the International Monetary Fund as well as regional blocs, most notably the European Union.

Some commentators went further and emphasised the ways in which there were parallel processes of cultural and social integration as common ideas and even *mores* seemed to engulf the globe. Against this background, it was said, the nation-state was losing its former economic and political importance. Trans-national and supra-national institutions were shaping the policies pursued by individual countries and there was an increasingly visible loss of national *sovereignty*.

Periodic crises did little to dent confidence in the logic of globalization. Nonetheless, as the 2008 to 2009 financial crisis took hold, that logic was placed in doubt. The liberalization of global finance and the creation of deep cross-national financial linkages laid a basis for contagion and the crisis spread rapidly from the US housing market to much of the developed world (Gedikli, Erdoğan and Yıldırım, 2015: 291). World trade dipped alarmingly. In December 2008, air cargo traffic was 23 per cent lower than a year later (*The Economist*, 2009). Indeed, the collapse in the volume of world trade was unprecedented in the post-war era. The only valid comparison was with developments following the Wall Street Crash and at the onset of the Great Depression (van Bergeijk, 2010: 8). The KOF Swiss Economic Institute (Konjunkturforschungsstelle) has constructed an index of globalization that distinguishes between economic, social and political variables. It concluded that the pace of economic and social globalization decelerated very significantly and the financial crisis had '... created a severe setback for the globalization process' (KOF Swiss Economic Institute, 2012).

There were expectations that, as in the 1930s, the crisis would inevitably lead countries towards the adoption of protectionist measures, particularly where alternative fiscal or monetary policy options were limited (van Bergeijk, 2010: 96-97). Although in the wake of the crisis countries generally eschewed formal protectionist measures, in the event they responded by adopting 'murky' measures including the use of health and safety regulations or 'buy-national' clauses in stimulus packages so as to discriminate against foreign suppliers. A study concluded that a fall in real GDP growth by a percentage point typically resulted in a 4.4 per cent increase in the number of newly implemented trade-restrictive measures (Georgiadis and Gräb,

2013: 13). Thus, there were solid reasons for thinking that globalization had stalled and processes of de-globalization might be taking place.

European strains

Under the weight of the crisis, and the painfully slow character of the subsequent recovery, some of the institutions that had come to symbolise globalization processes were thrown into crisis. Against this background, de-globalization increasingly acquired a political, as well as an economic, dimension.

In particular, there were profound strains within the European Union. The introduction of the euro (that became legal tender at the beginning of 2002) had, by reducing barriers to trade and exchange, held out the promise of much deeper economic integration among the member states that participated and the acceleration of economic growth. Although there had been an acknowledgement that a common monetary policy, (interest rates in the Eurozone are set by the European Central Bank), and a commitment to price stability implied moves towards a common fiscal policy and participating countries were required, on joining the euro, to limit the general government deficit to three per cent of GDP, there had been a degree of 'fudging' when countries were first accepted for membership. Furthermore, revenue collection procedures were in some member countries limited in scope and tax monies went uncollected. Even more importantly, the structural character of national economies in northern Europe and the Mediterranean countries were very different, and once hit by the economic crisis, budget deficits ballooned in countries such as Greece. European Union demands for fiscal rebalancing and 'austerity' through drastic public expenditure reductions brought the country to the edge of withdrawal from the Eurozone.

For parts of the left, the fate of Greece and the process by which it had to accommodate demands for expenditure reductions, whatever the social cost, highlighted the EU's inherent neoliberalism. Both Podemos, which won support from about a fifth of Spanish voters in 2015, and Jeremy Corbyn who became Labour leader in the UK, seemed ambiguous about the EU and were certainly critical of core EU policies. In the US, Vermont Senator Bernie Sanders, who challenged Hillary Clinton for the 2016 Democratic presidential nomination, campaigned against corporate outsourcing, offshoring and trade treaties pointing to the ways in which they, he asserted, benefitted elites, accelerated inequalities, threatened labour standards and the environment, and undermined democratic governance by creating investor-state dispute mechanisms.

The populist right and Brexit

It was, however, the populist right rather than the populist left that made much more of the political running.[1] In the June 2016 referendum, 51.9 per cent of UK voters backed Brexit, a cause largely championed by the United Kingdom Independence Party (UKIP) and the Conservative Party right.

Economics only constituted part, perhaps a relatively small part, of the overall picture during the referendum campaign. In the month preceding the vote, the Leave campaigners who were faced by claims that withdrawal from the EU would trigger an immediate economic collapse turned towards immigration and assertions that British sovereignty had been undermined. Their representations merged immigration from the EU's accession countries in the east together with anxieties about non-white refugees and migrants. Alongside claims that large amounts of funding could be transferred to the National Health Service, they held out the promise that migration would be curbed and the UK would again become an independent and prosperous trading nation. The importance of immigration in the campaign (it was identified as the single biggest reason for their vote by a third of Leave voters while a further 49 per cent pointed to sovereignty more broadly) quickly led both the major political parties to conclude after the vote that the free movement of labour, which had allowed large numbers to move to the UK, had to end. In practical terms, that meant that the UK had to leave the single market and the customs union as well as the EU itself. In contrast with the Swiss or Norwegian models, there had to be a 'hard' Brexit (Lord Ashcroft Polls, 2016).

The Brexit vote not only brought migration but broader populist discourses to the fore. Such discourses were structured around the restoration of national sovereignty and spoke in the name of the 'people' (a defining feature of populism) thereby laying the basis for anti-pluralism (insofar as others must necessarily be working against the people's interest) and hostility towards the economic, cultural and political openness that had seemingly characterised recent decades (Müller, 2016). In populist eyes, the 'people' are pitted against a globalizing elite and there are often hints of a mytholo-

---

1. There are however ideational overlaps between the left and right. At times, during the 2016 presidential election campaign, Senator Bernie Sanders and Donald Trump seemed to speak in similar terms about the consequences of trade liberalization. Furthermore, both left and right come together in pointing to the ways in which globalization constrains national sovereignty while at the same time asserting that individual countries can break free and determine their own fate (Richards, 2017: loc 920).

gised past (perhaps set in the 1950s) when nations were independent, homogenous and, it is invariably suggested, much more stable, ordered, and prosperous.

Even before the Brexit vote, right-wing, illiberal populist parties had made significant electoral gains. In the May 2014 elections to the European Parliament, UKIP won 26.6 per cent of the vote and the Front National (France) gained 24.9 per cent. In the 2015 Danish general election, Dansk Folkeparti (the Danish People's Party) secured 21.1 per cent of the vote thereby establishing itself as the country's second largest party. At the same time, some centre-right and centre-left parties shifted their policies so as to accommodate the new populism through, for example, an embrace of intensified migration controls.

Electing Donald Trump

There was a further and even more dramatic challenge to globalizing processes when Donald Trump was elected as US president in November 2016. Although the result had looked increasingly close in the final days of the campaign, Trump's victory in the Electoral College was largely unexpected. He won in part because he commanded the overwhelming support of long-term Republican voters. His margin of victory came, however, from former Democratic voters, predominantly white non-college graduates, who had backed Barack Obama in 2012 but switched four years later (CNN Exit Polls, 2016). They were disproportionately concentrated in the northeastern 'rustbelt' states that had once been hailed as Clinton's 'firewall'.

Such voters lived in communities that had gained little or nothing from the economic recovery. A Georgetown University study found that 95 per cent of the jobs created since the beginning of 2010 had gone to those with more than a high-school education (*Georgetown University Center on Education and the Workforce*, 2016). A sense of economic loss merged together with feelings of cultural dispossession and Trump's ability to campaign as an insurgent outsider.

Trump's election fuelled anxieties about de-globalization processes to a much greater extent than events in Europe. This was not only because of the US's weight in the world but also, he seemed to offer an even sharper break with mainstream politics. While the European populist parties championed 'soft' or 'hard' Euroscepticism, Trump's populism openly incorporated protectionism. During his campaign he called for a 45 per cent tariffs upon imports on China and announced that the country would be labelled a 'currency manipulator'. He demanded US withdrawal from efforts to ratify the Trans-Pacific Partnership (TPP) and the renegotiation of the North American Free Trade Agreement (NAFTA) which had brought together the

US, Canada and Mexico. Future trade agreements he said would be bilateral. Manufacturing employment would be restored and reinvigorated. Trump's slogan 'America First', proclaimed in his Inaugural Address, extended to both foreign and economic policy.

Turning the tide?

There were nonetheless signs, by mid-2017, that the de-globalizing tide might have begun to turn. Some economic indicators provided comfort. Although the rate of increase was markedly weaker than in the pre-crisis years, world trade (at market exchange rates) had grown at about the same rate as world GDP over a five-year period from 2011 (World Trade Organization, 2016). The KOF Swiss Economic Institute found that although there had been a slowdown in the pace of change, overall processes of globalization continued after the crisis. Indeed, in 2014, the increase in the KOF globalization index was the highest since 2007 (KOF Swiss Economic Institute, 2017).

There were also indications of a political shift. In particular, the election of Emmanuel Macron, who assertively celebrated the European ideal, as French president and the oddly inconclusive results of the UK general election, suggested that traditional politics were perhaps making a comeback. At the same time, beneath the surface dysfunctionality, the Trump administration and the Congressional Republicans pursued fairly well-established party objectives.

Nonetheless, while perhaps checked, right-wing populism was far from beaten. Although decisively defeated in the French presidential contest, Marine Le Pen, the Front National candidate, secured 34 per cent in the second round of the French presidential election, double the 17.2 per cent won by her father in 2002. UKIP was wiped off the electoral map in the 2017 UK general election, but the commitment to a 'hard Brexit' remained in place. Across the European Union efforts to widen and deepen the project seemed to have largely disappeared from the policy agenda. And, by mid-2018, the Trump administration had started to flex its populist muscles through the imposition of tariffs on China, the EU and the US's NAFTA partners thereby triggering fears of a trade war.

De-globalization in context

Nonetheless, a comprehensive picture of de-globalization, going beyond the simple charting of election results, requires that the concept of globalization itself is subjected to scrutiny.

Despite its wide usage and place in the popular vocabulary, globalization is in many ways an unsatisfactory term. It suggests a process that is far advanced, or even near completion, whereas nationally demarcated markets continue to be critically important for firms, consumers and state actors. There are, in reality, relatively few genuinely trans-national firms and multinational corporations are, for the most part, based in one individual country (Hirst and Thompson, 1996). Distance still matters insofar as trade and exchange are much more likely to take place between nations in relatively close proximity to each other. 'Globalization' is furthermore often used as an 'across-the-board' term that fails to distinguish between different rates of trans-national integration across different economic sectors. Some sectors have opened up to trans-national supply chains or are dominated by multinational, perhaps trans-national, firms, whereas others remain overwhelmingly national in character. In other words, there is *variegation*. Other commentators provide a different form of critique and argue that where there have been globalizing processes they constitute 'Americanization' rather than 'globalization' insofar as processes has been driven by, and have been subordinate to, US corporations and the hegemony of the dollar (Gowan, 1999). The concept of globalization has furthermore seemed to rest upon invocations of a past era when there were independent, self-contained national economies. However, the history of the British, French or Belgian empires, or the gold standard that regulated exchange rates before the early 1930s (and certainly in the era before 1914) suggest that the economic fate of individual countries was closely bound together at times in the past. Indeed, there may even have been more 'globalization' in earlier years.

In sum, because globalization always had a limited, partial and sectorally differentiated character, the term 'globalizing processes' is more appropriate. Furthermore, such de-globalizing processes should be seen as a set of incremental and variegated adjustments along sets of continuums rather than a dramatic macro-level shift.

Holding back

There are, furthermore, significant forces holding backing and containing those de-globalizing processes that may be taking place or might gather momentum in the years to come. First, as has been widely noted, the bonds holding trans-national relationships and some supranational institutions in place are more deeply embedded than in the 1930s when the building of autarkic, militarized and expansionary national economies contributed to trade wars and the eventual outbreak of the Second World War. In particular, there is evidence to suggest that the World Trade Organization is, because of its institutional structures, relatively resilient: '... its formally equal representation of interests ... helps keep the WTO in business by providing a positive incentive to stay within the system' (Chorev and Babb, 2009: 480). Despite suspensions and the building of border fences, the Schengen agreement, allowing free movement across borders, was still holding in 2017.

Furthermore, for the most part, continental European right-wing populism has sought to maximize national advantages and freedoms *within* the EU rather than seeking withdrawal. In other words, its commitment to the restoration of national sovereignty has been limited and conditional in character.

Second, while the western economies are to some degree being drawn towards populism, nationalism and protectionism, there have been very different responses in some other countries. This may owe as much to the different ways in which countries experienced globalization over the decades that preceded the financial crisis as to events from 2008 onwards. Joseph Stiglitz, the former Chair of the Council of Economic Advisers, argued that there was an important divide between countries such as those in east Asia that were able to manage globalization processes themselves that those that were subject to the 'market fundamentalism' of the International Monetary Fund and were as a consequence exposed to serious risk when the financial crisis broke (Stiglitz, 2015: 218). Certainly, in part because of the ways in which it steered its responses to globalization, China has now sought to champion trade liberalization. Chinese President Xi Jinping spoke in terms at the World Economic Forum in Davos that seemed to recall the traditions of Manchester liberalism: 'It is true that economic globalization has created new problems, but this is no justification to write off economic globalization altogether ... We must remain committed to developing free trade and investment' (quoted in Ehrenfreund, 2017). Having said that, under China's aegis, globalizing processes may take a rather different form given its inability to provide markets and institutions comparable with those in the US that provided a mainstay for the international order (Hu and Spence, 2017: 60).

Third, although mediated to some degree by race and ethnicity, there are also important generational differences regarding attitudes towards globalizing processes. In other words, such processes can draw upon a political constituency. In the wake of the 2017 UK general election, the polling organization *YouGov* hailed age as '... the new dividing line in British politics' (Curtis, 2017). Among those aged 18 and 19 who were first time voters, the Labour Party was forty-seven percentage points ahead of the Conservatives. By contrast, among those aged over 70, the Conservatives had a fifty-percentage point advantage (Curtis, 2017). While Labour formally shared the Conservatives' commitment to a 'hard Brexit' and an end to the free movement of workers, the party appears to have been seen as a vehicle for expressing anti-Brexit sentiments. A year earlier in the referendum, nearly three quarters (73%) of 18 to 24-year-olds voted for the UK to remain in the EU (Lord Ashcroft Polls, 2016). While turnout was about 64 per cent of registered voters aged 18 to 24, over 90 per cent of those aged over 65 voted, thereby giving the Leave campaign its vital edge (Helm, 2016). *The Daily Mirror* thus dubbed the 2017 election result as 'the revenge of the youth' (Bond and Robson, 2017). Of course it remains to be seen if this is a cohort effect or whether attitudes will change as young people age.

Fourth, business interests and the power that such interests exercise over policy-making processes should also be brought into the picture.[1] Power is not, of course, a straightforward concept. Jacob Hacker and Paul Pierson have drawn an important distinction between the *structural* and *instrumental* power of business (Hacker and Pierson, 2002: 280-286). Instrumental power refers to the use of political instruments such as lobbying, campaigning or contributions to candidates' election funds so as to secure access to policymakers or sway particular policy decisions.

For the most part, the evidence to date suggests that although there are important sectoral differences, business has not perceived the prospect of de-globalising processes as a serious or sustained challenge to its interests and has not sought to mobilize politically. Its *instrumental* power has not been deployed to any degree. In the US, some firms (such as Uber, Lyft and Airbnb as well as many of the tech companies) condemned or distanced themselves from President Trump's early efforts to restrict immigration, but business interests more broadly, and the stock market, were drawn to the administration's pledges to enact free market policies while at the same time seemingly disregarding or disbelieving the commitment to protectionism and the other populist themes in Trump's campaign rhetoric. Corporate executives from some of the country's biggest firms met with President Trump shortly after he took office and were reportedly wooed by the promise of lower corporate tax rates and reduced regulation (Lam, 2017).

If events in the UK are again considered, larger firms leant heavily towards the Remain camp but seem to have 'sat out' the Brexit referendum. 80 per cent of firms belonging to the Confederation of British Industry (CBI) supported continued EU membership while just five percent backed the Leave campaign (Inman, 2016). The small business sector, which might have been expected to see the EU as costly and burdensome, was evenly divided between those that supported Brexit (37 per cent) and Remainers (38 per cent) while significant numbers were uncertain or did not feel sufficiently informed about the issue (Farrell, 2016).

Nonetheless, despite these sentiments, relatively few firms or business leaders spoke out. The few exceptions included the Ryanair CEO, Michael O'Leary, who campaigned loudly against the prospect of Brexit, and pub chain JD Wetherspoon chairman, Tim Martin, and JCB's Anthony Bamford, who both actively backed the Leave side. There have been suggestions that these expressions of opinion were at least in part shaped by sectoral cleavages. Firms oriented towards the domestic market (such as pub and restaurant companies) or private companies (such as JCB) that did not have to fear the stock market crash that, it was anticipated, would follow in the wake of a Leave vote, were more likely to perceive the EU in negative terms.

Why, then, did business not do more to challenge Brexit? In part, there was a widely-shared belief ahead of the referendum that the Remain camp would win. There may also have been a fear that a firm's brand might be damaged or compromised by taking sides. And, for many, EU membership represented a difficult and unclear trade-off between potential export opportunities and its perceived cost and regulatory burdens.

Further de-globalizing processes, for example the realities of Brexit and particularly the prospect of a 'hard Brexit', may, however, bring business interests into the political arena. It might be argued that in such circumstances, they will act as a barrier impeding de-globalization and efforts to reconstruct the sovereignty of the nation-state. Certainly, some sectors, most notably the City of London, fear that withdrawal from the single market will lead to the withdrawal of 'passporting' rights and the ability of financial institutions to trade freely across the continent.

Against this background, the British government may become subject to instrumental power through lobbying and more acutely sensitized to the *structural* power of business interests. This form of power is derived from Charles Lindblom's assertion that business holds an inherently privileged position (Lindblom, 1977). That privilege is rooted in the importance of firms in driving economic growth upon which, in turn, employment and prosperity depend. In contrast with instrumental power, structural power is 'automatic' and embedded within the assumptions of policymakers. Few, if any, contemporary governments risk defying business interests in any sustained or decisive way. There is always an implicit understanding that policy decisions perceived as 'anti-business' will dent confidence, are likely to trigger a fall in share prices or the exchange rate and may thus lead to corporate disinvestment.

There were signs that business was reminding the newly re-elected Conservative government of its structural capacities in mid-2017 as the early Brexit negotiations got off to a seemingly slow and rocky start. Fearful that the U.K. might have to leave the EU without any form of free trade agreement, the CBI and other business groupings called for the country to remain indefinitely within the single market and the customs union until such an agreement was concluded (Roberts, 2017). The Brexit plan unveiled by the British government in July 2018 seemed to recognize the need to assuage business interests insofar as it called for an EU – UK free trade area covering goods.

The white working-class

All these factors will shape the extent, scale and character of de-globalizing processes in the western countries. They will also rest upon the politics of the white working-class. In the US, as noted above, it was the defection of white non-college graduates that gave Trump his margin of victory. In the Brexit vote, support for withdrawal from the EU was most strongly backed (64 per cent) among social classes C2 and DE who were those on the lowest rungs of the economic ladder (Lord Ashcroft Polls, 2016).

The shift among significant layers of the white working-class, once bound to social democracy in Europe and the Democratic Party in the US, towards the populist right may lead to political reconfiguration. Neoliberalism, which had championed limited government, free markets and free trade may have to make its peace with demands for trade restrictions and greater social protection. President Trump navigates his way between these different philosophies. In the UK, Theresa May seemed to be remaking the Conservative Party around the new populism. In celebrated remarks after becoming Prime Minister, she seemed to speak out against internationalism and globalism:

'Today, too many people in positions of power behave as though they have more in common with international elites than with the people down the road, the people they employ, the people they pass on the street ... But if you believe you are a citizen of the world, you are a citizen of nowhere. You don't understand what citizenship means' (quoted in Bearak, 2016).

There was a later retreat from this form of rhetoric but there is nonetheless likely to becontinued jostling between globalizing and de-globalizing processes at both an economic and political level. Right-wing populism is far from a spent force. In an era of professionalized politics, politicians and campaigns offering few distinctive choices, the 'outsider' has an instinctive appeal for those who feel distanced from policy processes. Much will depend upon the ability of mainstream politics to address the anguish that has spurred populist forces, overall rates of economic growth and the capacity of the western economies to reintegrate those who feel they have lost far too much.

References

Bearak, Max (2016). 'Theresa May criticized the term 'citizen of the world.' But half the world identifies that way', *The Washington Post*, 5 October, https://www.washingtonpost.com/news/worldviews/wp/2016/10/05/theresa-may-criticized-the-term-citizen-of-the-world-but-half-the-world-identifies-that-way/?utm_term=.be802b42745c

Bello, Walden (2002). Deglobalization: Ideas for a New World Economy, Zed Books.

Bond, Anthony and Steve Robson (2017). 'Revenge of the youth! How 18 to 24-year-olds furious over Brexit gave Theresa May a disastrous general election result', *The Daily Mirror*, 9 June, http://www.mirror.co.uk/news/politics/youth-vote-swing-it-pundits-10589161

Chorev, Nitsan and Sarah Babb (2009). 'The crisis of neoliberalism and the future of international institutions: A comparison of the IMF and the WTO', *Theory & Society*, 38:459-484.

CNN Exit Polls (2016). *Exit Polls*, 23 November, http://edition.cnn.com/election/results/exit-polls

Curtis, Chris (2017). 'How Britain voted at the 2017 general election', *YouGov*, 13 June, https://yougov.co.uk/news/2017/06/13/how-britain-voted-2017-general-election/

The Economist (2009). 'Turning their backs on the world', *The Economist*, 19 February, http://www.economist.com/node/13145370

Ehrenfreund, Max (2017). 'World leaders find hope for globalization in Davos amid populist revolt', *The Washington Post*, 17 January, https://www.washingtonpost.com/news/wonk/wp/2017/01/17/chinese-president-warns-against-trade-war-in-davos/?utm_term=.6dc0a8f7ac40

Farrell, Sean (2016). 'UK small businesses are evenly split on Brexit, poll says', *The Guardian*, 2 June, https://www.theguardian.com/business/2016/jun/02/uk-small-businesses-are-evenly-split-on-brexit-poll-says

Georgetown University Center on Education and the Workforce (2016). *America's Divided America: College Haves and Have-Nots*, Washington DC: Georgetown University Center on Education and the Workforce.
https://cew.georgetown.edu/cew-reports/americas-divided-recovery/

Georgiadis, G and J Gräb (2013). 'Growth, real exchange rates and trade protectionism since the financial crisis', *ECB Working Paper* 1618.

Hacker, Jacob, and Paul Pierson (2002). 'Business Power and Social Policy: Employers and the Formation of the American Welfare State', *Politics and Society* 30: 277-325.

Helm, Toby (2016). 'EU referendum: youth turnout almost twice as high as first thought', *The Observer*, 10 July, https://www.theguardian.com/politics/2016/jul/09/young-people-referendum-turnout-brexit-twice-as-high

Gedikli, Ayfer, Seyfettin Erdoğan and Durmuş Çağrı Yıldırım (2015). 'After The Global Crisis, Is It Globalization or Globalonelization?', in Özlem Olgu, Hasan Dinçer and Ümit Hacıoğlu, *Handbook of Research on Strategic Developments and Regulatory Practice in Global Finance*, IGI Global, 287-307.

Gowan, Peter (1999). *The Global Gamble: Washington's Faustian Bid for World Dominance*, Verso.

Hirst, Paul and Grahame Thompson (1996). *Globalization in Question: The International Economy and the Possibilities of Governance*, Polity Press.

Hu, Fred and Michael Spence (2017). 'Why Globalization Stalled and How to Restart It', *Foreign Affairs*, July / August, 96:4, 54-63.

Inman, Phillip (2016). 'CBI member survey reveals huge support for remaining in EU', *The Guardian*, 15 March, https://www.theguardian.com/business/2016/mar/15/cbi-member-survey-reveals-huge-support-for-remaining-in-eu

KOF Swiss Economic Institute (2012). 'Press Release – KOF Index of Globalization 2012: Economic Crisis Brings Economic Globalization to Fall', *KOF Swiss Economic Institute*, 16 March, http://globalization.kof.ethz.ch/media/filer_public/2013/03/25/press_release_2012_en.pdf

KOF Swiss Economic Institute (2017). 'KOF Index of Globalization 2017: Netherlands Are the Most Globalized Country', *KOF Swiss Economic Institute*, 20 April, https://www.kof.ethz.ch/en/news-and-events/media/press-releases/2017/04/kof-glo balization-index-2017.html

Lam, Bourree (2017). 'Trump's promises to corporate leaders: lower taxes and fewer regulations', *The Atlantic*, 23 January, https://www.theatlantic.com/business/archive/ 2017/ 01/trump-corporate-tax-cut/514148/

Lindblom, Charles (1977). *Politics and Markets*, Basic Books.

Lord Ashcroft Polls (2016). 'How the United Kingdom voted on Thursday ... and why', Lord Ashcroft Polls, 24 June, http://lordashcroftpolls.com/2016/06/how-the-united-kingdom-voted-and-why/

Müller, Jan-Werner (2016). *What is Populism?* University of Pennsylvania Press.

Richards, Steve (2017). *The Rise of the Outsiders: How Mainstream Politics Lost its Way*, Atlantic Books.

Roberts, Dan (2017). 'UK business leaders to call for indefinite delay in leaving single market', *The Guardian*, 6 July, https://www.theguardian.com/politics/2017/jul/06/uk-business-leaders-to-call-for-indefinite-delay-in-leaving-single-market?CMP=Share_iOSApp_Other

Stiglitz, Joseph (2015). 'Globalism's Discontents', in Frank J Lechner and John Boli (eds.), *The Globalization Reader*, Wiley-Blackwell, 218-226.

van Bergeijk, Peter A.G. (2010). *On the Brink of Deglobalization*, Edward Elgar.

World Trade Organization (2016). 'Trade growth to remain subdued in 2016 as uncertainties weigh on global demand', *World Trade Organization*, 7 April, https:// www.wto.org/english/news_e/pres16_e/pr768_e.htm

Business Case for Europe

By Leif Beck Fallesen, Economic and business commentator,
Former editor of Børsen, Chairman of DIS board

A Stronger Business Case for Europe

From Sell to Buy. In just a couple of years the business case for the European Union has changed dramatically from an almost unanimous strong Sell, to a Buy mode, albeit with some hedging. Politically, the messy Brexit divorce and political turmoil at the European and national levels have nourished the perception, not just in the media, of the European Union as a basket case on the verge of implosion. But this verdict is premature and incorrect, and the business case is more optimistic. Donald Trump and Vladimir Putin are catalysts of more political integration, not less, as the EU responds to challenges to freedom of trade and national security.

The European Union grew at a faster pace than the U.S. in 2017, and the political climate has improved sharply with Emmanuel Macron as the strongest pro-EU and reformist president in France in decades. In Germany, chancellor Angela Merkel and her SPD coalition will not be willing and able to endorse all of Macron's visions of economic and monetary union, but the structures and functions of the Eurozone will become stronger. The combination of benign economics and political alignment between the two major shareholders of the European Union, Germany and France, have historically been a harbinger of more economic integration. This time there are stronger headwinds, generated by populist parties in almost all member countries, but progress is on the cards.

The European Union has survived the financial crisis and its Greek sequel. Brexit has not triggered a collapse but has reinvigorated French and German determination to save the European Union from breaking up. This is a unique window of opportunity for the European Union to respond and move forward, not to a United States of Europe, but to a political and economic entity that will be stronger than before the financial crisis. In the long term this will benefit European business and all international investors, not least American companies selling to high-end consumers and corporations. Short term there will be confrontation in the digital economy, as the EU attempts to establish a level playing field in a game that is dominated by U.S. and, increasingly, Asian giants.

A compass is a useful instrument for navigation, and the European Union needs a really good compass to move forward, whatever the destination. It is a difficult course to chart, because the European Union must master major challenges from all four compass directions at the same time. Failure is not an option, but it is certainly a risk. Especially as the final destination is in dispute by those on board.

Europe is forced to respond to major challenges from all four compass directions at the same time. If Europe fails to cope, it will be at the mercy of decisions taken outside its control. The consequences may be dire, and fatal to the European Union as we know it. It is also the worst possible scenario for not just European business, but for the global economy.

The challenge from the West can be summarized in one name: Donald Trump. The United States is the European Union's most important partner in trade and global politics, and the President is compromising both, and his unpredictability is anathema to business. That said, Donald Trump could have been an - unwilling - candidate for European of the Year 2017, if such a title existed. No other statesman has done more to unite the Europeans in 2017. Trump's rapidly unfolding trade war will have a similar effect in 2018 and in 2019, when the impact on global economic growth will be visible.

Trump's campaign predictions of the collapse of the euro and the European Union have been watered down, like his views on NATO and Russia, with a little help from Vladimir Putin. Trump has united many Europeans in the conviction that the European Union must move forward. For business and political leaders alike, Trump is unpredictable and, many would add, irresponsible. His ability to handle geopolitical risks, including North Korea, is very much in doubt. Unleashing a trade war could cause the perfect storm in global financial markets and derail the strongest global economic surge since the financial crisis in 2008.

One word summarises the challenge from the South: immigrants. In truth, it is misleading, as two words are really needed, immigrants and refugees. But it has proven impossible to identify and thus separate the two groups, and hence the policy response, deterring entry and attempting repatriation, is the same. Despite a tradition of open doors for political refugees in most European Union countries, even the most open of all, Germany and Sweden, have been overwhelmed by the numbers.

Germany's Angel Merkel famously said 'Wir schaffen das' (We can handle this) when the numbers started rising. But more than a million newcomers in 2015 forced her to change her policy, aptly renamed 'Wir schaffen das nicht' (We can't handle his) by irreverent commentators. Some countries erected physical barriers, and governments everywhere have set limits on immigration, even refusing to participate in any fair sharing of refugees stranded in the entry countries of Greece and Italy. Immigration, or rather stopping immigration, became the unrivalled political issue, exploited by populist parties. Angela Merkel had to accept a cap on numbers in her coalition after an election in 2017 with heavy losses for her party and a first time (federal) parliamentary presence of the anti-immigrant AfD party.

A deal with Turkey stopped the exodus to Greece, and in 2017 the total number of immigrants and refugees were back at the more manageable level prior to the surge in 2015. But Italy is still facing a massive illegal immigration challenge, sheltering 600,000 immigrants other EU countries have refused to accommodate, and a lack of EU solidarity that had a strong influence on the outcome of the Italian elections in 2018. Two populist and Eurosceptic parties won the most votes, and though the wave of support for populist parties seems to have culminated in 2017, the Italian, Austrian and Hungarian election results show that is too early to write the obituary of populism in the European Union. Poland is on collision course with the fundamental democratic rights in the European Union, despite being the best economic performer over ten years.

European business is paying a price. If there is a new surge in immigration, it is almost certain that border controls will be re-introduced, eliminating one of the big advantages of the single market in the European Union. Already a major challenge, attracting the skilled workers and specialists that European businesses need to grow, will become harder. Denmark is an illuminating case. More than 10% of the working population in the private sector in Denmark are non-Danes. Current production cannot be maintained without these economic immigrants, and in an ageing society more will be needed to secure future growth. The situation is similar in most member states of the European Union.

One man, Vladimir Putin, is the personification of the challenge from East. He is given responsibility for the continued application of the dirty tricks of his former espionage trade in the KGB, targeting a former double agent with nerve gas in the United Kingdom in early 2018, perhaps only one of many. Putin's annexation of the Crimea and proxy intervention in Ukraine had already triggered sanctions, and the current escalation has already been labelled a new Cold War. Justified or not, there is fear that the ethnic Russian minorities in the Baltic countries could, at some date, provide a pretext for, if not military intervention, then rhetoric and posturing that would undermine business confidence and economic growth. All European Union member states bordering the Baltic Sea are now spending more on defence, and military co-operation between NATO members and non-members has strengthened.

From a business perspective, a Cold War began years ago. It may now become even colder and costlier. Trade with Russia is far more important to the European Union than it is to the United States, and current and potential lost business is much greater, which is why German business in particular is adamant that sanctions against Russia do not continue to escalate.

Energy is a major issue, symbolised by a second Russian gas pipeline to Germany, planned to pass through Danish territorial waters. It is opposed by critics who claim that it will increase EU energy dependence on Russia. Critics include Poland, the Ukraine, the Baltic countries and the U.S. Congress, while Germany insists it needs the gas to replace the nuclear energy that is being phased out. The pipeline may likely be rerouted at greater cost but remains a divisive issue in the attempts to establish a European single energy market.

The challenge from the North is more fluid: the melting Arctic ice cap. It is visible proof of climate change, even as U.S. president Donald Trump remains in denial, and the U.S. exits from the Paris international climate agreement. This shifts responsibility for global leadership in dealing with climate change to the European Union. That mantle is accepted by a significant majority of voters, politicians and business leaders, and green policies are being ambitiously implemented at the city, national and European levels, sustained by better finances and a belief that they are the source of future jobs,

This makes a strong European business case for investing in green industries and products. Not just for green industry itself, such as the producers of wind turbines, but for industry in general. Government support is still important, in many cases crucial, to the business case for investment in green industries. But demand for more climate friendly products and productions is now market driven globally. There are still European industries that find it difficult to adapt to this transformation – chemicals are, not surprisingly, one them – but by most it is considered to be either unavoidable or a future global competitive advantage. Some will say both.

The melting ice cap is not just fostering new green business opportunities; it opens vast new geographical spaces for exploration and exploitation. Fossil fuels may not be desirable for environmental reasons, but oil will be around for a long time. Greenland hopes to discover existing oil and rare minerals in commercially viable quantities. If these hopes materialize, Greenland may not be alone. New discoveries elsewhere would likely exacerbate existing conflicts over boundaries and rights to resources in the Arctic.

These new business opportunities come with a political risk that will make some investors wary. The Arctic is an obvious candidate for more confrontation with Russia, and Greenland is courting Chinese investment and seeking independence from

Denmark as soon as its finances permit. The elections in April 2018 confirmed this ambition.

The responses of the core to the challenges from all compass directions will determine the future of business, economic growth and political coherence in the European Union. Due diligence of current global competitiveness of European business could be a start. The first result is an acceptable pass. The trade balance is in surplus, driven by the very strong German export performance in all global markets. The European Union has pulled out of the financial crisis and is growing at a faster rate than expected a few years ago, though this momentum may not be maintained if global markets become less free.

But the United States responded faster and more effectively in 2008 crisis, and Greece is still in the process of exiting economic intensive care, and the country has suffered extreme social costs as a consequence of unnecessarily strict austerity policies. Unemployment, especially youth unemployment, is still high across most of southern Europe. Thus, European Union economic governance will only be given a passing grade by the northern member states. Austerity policies succeeded, but the patient almost died on the operating table.

Business has a vested interest in a core that can deliver. The track record is not good, and governments have usurped the many of the powers of the institutions of the European Union. But output is what matters to business, not the institutional framework of decision-making. While understandable, the future business environment very much depends on what happens in the political architecture and balance of power in the European Union. From a business perspective, they are better than they were a few years ago. Assuming that business desires economic growth, business friendly policies, fair competition, and a level playing field, including taxes. Global companies with high market shares and low effective tax rates, with American high-tech giants as archetypes, although they are not alone, would not agree with this generalization. But they may be well be forced to take it or leave it.

One change in the political architecture is inevitable. The United Kingdom will be leaving the core. Another change is equally inevitable. The Eurozone will spearhead European integration and economic governance, though not by naming a Eurozone Finance Minister or fathering a European Monteray Fund, as proposed by French President Emmanuel Macron. But some pooling of sovereignty – read commitment to financial transfers - will be implemented. France wants more pooling than Germany, and there will be work in progress for some time. Germany is adamant that it should not be called upon to pay for less prudent member states in a coming crisis, but more technical solutions can probably be designed to share risk.

The Eurozone already has a common monetary policy, administered by an independent central bank, the ECB, which, in practice, has been just as supportive of growth as the Federal Reserve has been, though its mandate is restricted to fighting inflation. It is noteworthy that the European Central Bank makes its decisions based on one man one vote, and the German board member has consistently opposed ECB policies, and has just as consistently been outvoted.

The real test of the new version of economic and monetary union, and how it performs in the next financial crisis, is yet to come. Time will tell. Optimists believe the odds are very good. They note that growth rates and employment have recovered, that budget deficits have been reined in, that that banks are better capitalized and better run than they were before the crisis, even though full banking union is on hold.

Pessimists retort that generals are often fighting the last wars, not the next one. Subprime mortgages in California and other U.S. states ignited and almost devoured the U.S. and European banking systems and triggered the worst economic crisis in fifty years. No one has come forward with a credible scenario of the next crisis much less a time frame. Pragmatists will argue that this not only requires a crystal ball, but decision-makers and markets who believe in crystal balls. Both are in short supply.

Outputs and decisions are what matter to business; some are by necessity immediate political responses to events in and outside the European Union, but most are, or claim to be, based on policies and commitments with a longer time frame. At least four commitments – 1) to free trade; 2) to a greener economy; 3) to digital governance; and 4) to a more socially responsible capitalism – are supported by a very broad political majority in the European Union. They define the business environment in the European Union but are arguably European comparative advantages, as they represent trends in the global economics and politics and may give European business the advantage of the first mover effect.

1) A commitment to free trade. The flagship of global free trade, Britain, is leaving the European Union, but, led by Germany, the North European member countries remain committed to free trade. All these economies are export-driven and globally competitive, and America First has no counterparty in the European Union. Even France, with a less globally competitive economy, historically protectionist and with hallmark national(ist) industrial policies within the European Union, has changed. President Emmanuel Macron has accepted mergers of the train industry of French Alsthom and German Siemens, accepting Siemens control of a much stronger European player. He has also accepted a merger of French STX and Italian shipyards, giving Fincantieri, the Italian shipyard, control of the merged com-

pany, with guarantees that it will continue building warships for the French Navy.

2) A commitment to the environment. Unlike the U.S. there is a very broad political consensus in Europe supporting regulation, public procurement and tax policies that constitute not only an ambitious environmental policy, but effectively an effective industrial policy. It holds the promise of new jobs to replace those lost to globalization and automation. Production of diesel cars will cease in Germany in a few years, nuclear power is disappearing in Germany, and there are probably more Teslas in Copenhagen than in any city in the world of similar size. At the European level the European Commission is trying to forge a new battery strategy, and all of Germany's expertise in cars is now targeting electric vehicles.

3) A commitment to market-oriented digital governance. The European Union is making a major effort to define rules that ensure fair competition and fair taxation in the digital economy. Broadband penetration in the European Union is high, most unions and employers accept digitalization and robots as a key to competitiveness and survival of jobs in manufacturing, with the unions demanding and obtaining support for training of redundant workers. The public sector is in the vanguard. In Denmark, all communication between government and citizens, both at the national and local level, is now online, and e-government is advancing rapidly.

At the European Union level, the charge for freer digital markets is led by a Dane. The Danish European Commissioner, Margrethe Vestager, is seen by many Americans, with good reason, as the scourge of U.S. high-tech companies, fining the likes of Google and Amazon billions of dollars for dodging taxes in the European Union by declaring their income in Ireland and elsewhere. Ireland is the very unusual and intuitively incomprehensible situation being forced to accept taxes it does not want to receive. Ireland prefers to safeguard its attraction as a de facto tax haven. Taxation of multinationals has always been a political issue in Europe, but the rapid ascent of e-commerce, controlled by American giants, have raised the stakes. Profits in national markets are hard to verify, and thus to tax. A simple tax on turnover has hitherto been turned down by a majority of European Union members.

Taxation is not a new issue. Neither is competition. What is new is the volume of digital services and physical products sold digitally. Physical products and data pose similar and yet very different challenges to competition law. The objective is the same, to ensure free competition without punishing companies that are big simply because they are better. In terms of market domination, the U.S. digital giants Amazon, Google and Facebook have, at least in Europe, been compared to the seven sisters, the U.S. oil majors whose cartel was dismantled by U.S. authorities in the 1920s to create fairer competition.

In the U.S. this argument has little traction today, but the European Union is seeking ways and means to do something. Google has reacted by making changes in its search engine. And the Facebook sandal in early 2018, when Cambridge Analytica had access to Facebook data, highlights the need to legally define who owns data and how they may be distributed. The new European Union data privacy legislation became effective in May 2018, and more may follow and set a global standard, despite opposition from Facebook, fearful of its business model.

4) A commitment to a more socially responsible incarnation of capitalism. The European Union has not produced a new definition of capitalism, but it is developing standard benchmarks of business behaviour over a wide range of issues. CSR – Corporate Social Responsibility – is stretched beyond relations between corporations and societies, questioning how welfare states should operate and be paid for, if and when the digital economy makes millions not just redundant, but unemployable.

The sophistication of U.S. financial markets used to be the envy of business and investors in the European Union. Shareholder value, the pursuit of short term profit, was the lodestar of American capitalism and IPOs, and initial public offerings were seen as a key driver of the Anglo-Saxon model of successful capitalism. Venture capital is more readily available, and U.S. business funds most of their needs on the capital market, bypassing the banks. In the European Union banks are still the main source of finance, which was an aggravating factor in Europe in the crash of 2008. The European Union still needs to develop its capital market, creating a capital union.

The digital economy has not created mass unemployment, at least not yet, but it has changed the labour market. Growth and job creation have come back after the crisis, but relatively far fewer highly paid jobs have been created. Outsourcing continues, more jobs are replaced by robots and automation, and inequality is rising. The fact that 40 percent of the German population had seen no growth in living standards for 10 years or more became a major issue in the German elections in 2017.

And inequality is not just a political and moral issue. Rising inequality reduces demand in an economy and many international organisations warn that it reduces growth in all major markets. Dealing with inequality is not easy.

Many Americans, and many conservatives, claim that there is no problem, it is simply the outcome of a free market in a free society. Social mobility will open the door to a better future for the individual and create more wealth for society. Inequality is an incentive fuelling a dynamic economy. Others regard the rising inequality as the inevitable collateral damage of globalization.

Critics have a very different narrative. Poverty is caused by the failure of capitalism, a society that deprives the individual of the means to find a job, and the means to live decently until a job is available. Socialists, and some famous U.S. billionaires, insist that society as a consequence must provide a minimum standard of living to the unemployed and implement economic policies that create jobs that a market economy obviously could not create without government intervention.

There is a fear that this time capitalism, globalization, will never be able to deliver the well-paid jobs needed, even in a strong global economic recovery such as 2017. Redundant workers have become unemployable and will become so even if the speed of technological change accelerates. Theoretically, the service sector could or should pick up the slack, but there must be sufficient demand for services, and money to pay for them.

President Barack Obama raised the minimum wage in the United States, and the same policy lever has been used in Europe. The European Commission advocates that all member states in the European Union should have a minimum wage as part of their social policies, though not the same wage for all member countries. Denmark has opted out of the European Union social policy, and wages are determined by collective bargaining. There is no legal minimum wage, but Denmark does have a proxy for a minimum income, a welfare state with flexicurity, and a safety net for those not covered by flexicurity.

The welfare states in the Nordic countries have provided a high standard of living, low unemployment, social security, strong public finances and global competitiveness. It is not by chance that it is seen as a role model by French President Emmanuel Macron in his attempt to reform the French economy. The welfare state de facto provides a minimum income, the equivalent of the minimum wage being discussed globally. But there have also been far-reaching reforms in the Nordic welfare states.

Fifty years ago, it was possible for a Dane to receive unemployment benefits indefinitely, and then retire seamlessly with a lifetime public pension. The equivalent of a minimum income for life, with no work required. Few exploited this opportunity, and it has evaporated. The focus is now on giving the unemployed the skills they need to find jobs, helped by the fact that it is increasingly considered socially stigmatizing not to have a job.

There is a fear that this time capitalism, globalization, will never be able to deliver the well paid jobs needed, even in a strong global economic recovery like 2017. Redundant workers have become unemployable, and will become even so if the speed of technological change accelerates. Theoretically, the service sector could or should pick up the slack, but there must be sufficient demand for services. A minimum income would not necessarily be spent on services, but demographics will generate growing demand for health and social services.

President Barack Obama raised the minimum wage in the United States, and the same policy lever has been used in Europe. The European Commission advocates that all member states in the European Union should have a minimum wage as part of their social policies, though not the same wage for all member countries. Denmark has opted out of the European Union social policy, and wages are determined by collective bargaining. There is no legal minimum wage. But Denmark does have a proxy for a minimum income, a welfare state with flexicurity, and a safety net for those not covered by flexicurity.

From a global business point of view, the Danish flexicurity model, the most stringent of the Nordic welfare models, is interesting because it clearly defines the role of business, unions and government. Business leaders should run their business as efficiently as they can. Hiring the staff they need, but no more, and letting them go immediately when they are no longer needed, even for short periods, without legal and union-negotiated restrictions common elsewhere. Wages are negotiated with unions, but the same wages are paid to non-unionized workers. Unionisation is not a legal requirement, but unions have the right to strike to get a wage agreement.

Business provides jobs, but not job security. The welfare state does not provide jobs, but financial security. This Danish model has combined the competitive advantages of free markets with social responsibility, and Danish exports are competitive on par with Germany. It is being emulated elsewhere in Europe, but it requires that voters are prepared to pay high taxes to finance a welfare state – which is not exactly on the Trump agenda – but it is also difficult to implement in southern Europe.

If global capitalism mutates towards a model sharing of some, if not all, of the four commitments of the European Union, this will obviously be a comparative advantage for European business. It is a very big 'if', with Donald Trump at the helm in the United States and an assertive China. But a patchwork may emerge featuring some of the commitments. There is wide support, at state level in the United States, for the European Union's green policies. China fights for free trade, with caveats, and much catch-up to be done on the domestic market. American digital giants aside, companies all over the world support the European Union's attempt to provide a regulatory framework for a freer digital economy.

The jury is still out. But if nothing is done to deal with the social collateral fallout from globalization and capitalism, populist parties will stir and profit from social and political turmoil all over the world, which will be the worst possible outcome for business, not just in the European Union, but globally.

It would not be fair to conclude without briefly mentioning some of the comparative disadvantages of the European Union. One, demographics, is not changing any time soon. Europe has an ageing population and immigrants that do not have the skills that business needs. High taxes make it difficult to attract top brains and skilled immigrants, and all immigrants face political hurdles. The U.S. is a much younger society.

Entrepreneurship is also at a comparative disadvantage. Europe has no Silicon Valley, though several wannabes, and there is still a historical stigma on failure that not only is a cultural barrier for young talent, but also limits available finance. There are signs of positive change, however, as politicians prioritise support of entrepreneurship – but cultural change takes time.

Defence procurement gives U.S. industry a very strong competitive advantage. The sheer size of the U.S. armed forces and, compared to Europe, the high priority of defence spending, has given the U.S. defence industry a technological lead not just in ordnance, but a lead that spills into in civilian production in many sectors, not least IT and aerospace. European defence procurement is much smaller, and the technology transfer to civilian production is thus proportionally smaller. The European Union is spending more on defence and reorganising defence procurement, but the gap against the U.S. remains huge.

The bottom line. The business case for Europe for the European Union is promising, and much better than it was a few years ago. Despite the appearance of a seemingly endless series of political crises, there is an underlying and improving business case for investing in a future for Europe. The economies are not only stronger than before the financial crisis but are adapting to greener and more digital future. The Eurozone will become a stronger driver of political integration in Europe, not giving birth to a United States of Europe, but a stronger European Union.

Perhaps there could be a backlash to a too optimistic view of the response of the European Union to these challenges. Populism is still strong in Europe, especially in Eastern Europe, Spain and Italy. For the time being populism may be on hold, or contained, in France, the Netherlands, Germany and the Nordic countries, but if the next economic crisis finds the European Union unable to cope with the next recession, then populist parties could set a political agenda that would cripple business. Success is by no means guaranteed for the business case for Europe. But no business cases have such a guarantee.

Export Financing

By Jørn Fredsgaard Sørensen, Director, Country, Bank and Sector Risk, Eksport Kredit Fonden EKF

Introduction

Credit is as old as money. Actually, credit probably precedes money, as it is difficult to imagine the existence of money without the notion of credit. Money probably arose based on IOUs, given in connection with trades where one party couldn't match the value of a purchased good with goods or precious metals of a similar value. Hence, the purchaser issued an IOU to the seller; a promise to deliver the person in possession of the IOU the remaining amount of value at a later date. In effect, the purchaser got credit from the seller.

To the extent that IOUs were issued by trustworthy persons or institutions (really a *sine qua non*, underlined by the fact that the origin of the word credit is from the Roman *credere*, to trust or to believe), they could be used in other transactions in which the original issuer did not take part. When used like this, the IOUs became money – and credit thus precedes money.

Credit is actually more than the origin of money. Credit is also the lubricant that makes a lot of everyday trade possible. Apart from cash transactions, where the full purchase amount is paid at the time of the transaction, credit is an integral part of all trades. It is very normal in most business-to-business transactions, that the balance of the purchase amount falls due at the end of the month, effectively giving the buyer up to 30 days credit. Any goods seller that in this way is obliged to provide credit to his customers will experience a negative cash flow in his business, unless he is able to force his own suppliers to provide him credit to at least the same extent that he is giving his customers.

Often, a bank is needed to provide a working capital facility that supplies the liquidity that closes the gaps with negative cash in the business. And if the business thrives, the company might ask for a term loan to finance some investments in capital equipment that expands the production capacity.

Export credit guarantees oil the wheels of international trade

1. A buyer needs financing to pay for his deliveries from an exporter in another country.
2. The buyer's own bank – or another bank active in the field of export credits – provides a loan to the buyer, which is used to pay the exporter.
3. A guarantee from the Export Credit Agency (ECA) in the exporter's country secures the bank against non-payment. In case the loan is large and with a long repayment period (tenor), the bank might also receive funding from the ECA to match the loan provided to the buyer.

The way export credits work

The same mechanisms take place in trade across borders. For smaller quantities of consumer goods, the sellers can provide credit, but for larger transactions, the sellers cannot act like banks to their customers (providing credits, in effect loans) – a real bank is needed to provide financing to the buyers.

Naturally, extending credits and loans to foreign entities entails more risks than doing the same with a domestic entity, whom might be known to the financier and from whom it will be easier to call in the instalment amounts when due. Hence the need for credit insurance.

Private trade credit insurance was born at the end of the nineteenth century, a natural development in this first era of globalization. Today, the private trade credit insurance market is quite concentrated, with three groups accounting for the vast majority of the market:

- Euler Hermes, part of the Allianz Group and the world's largest credit insurance provider

- Coface, formerly a French government sponsored institution, now part of the Natixis group
- Atradius, created as a merger between NCM and Gerling Kreditversicherung, now part of Grupo Catalana Occidente.

History and international regulation

Officially supported export credit guarantees – the main topic of this article – came into being in 1919 with the creation of the Export Credit Guarantee Department (ECGD) in Britain.[1] Within a decade, official export credit agencies (ECAs) were founded in Denmark, France, Belgium, Spain and Italy. This development can be explained with the inter-war period's less benign trading environment - in stark contrast to the rapid increase in world trade before World War I. Whereas world trade volumes increased almost fivefold from 1865 to 1913 (about 3.2 % p.a.), global trade expanded at an average annual pace of just 0.8% p.a. in the years 1914 to 1950. Before World War I, Europe, and in particular Britain, dominated world trade and less than a quarter of global merchandise trade occurred between non-European countries.[2]

After World War I, other European nations threatened Britain's dominant position and trade increasingly occurred with countries further away. In this environment, nations found it in their interest to support their domestic industries with guarantees against non-payment from foreign buyers.

After the meagre interwar years, trade picked up again after the end of World War II, particularly due to the post-war financial architecture based mainly on the ideas developed by the UK's John Maynard Keynes and the US' Harry Dexter White. The ideas were institutionalised at the Bretton Woods conference in 1944, where the World Bank and the International Monetary Fund were established.

However, the Bretton Woods delegates could not agree to establish the International Trade Organization (ITO). Instead, the less ambitious General Agreement on Tariffs and Trade (GATT) was adopted. Only in 1995 was the World Trade Organization (WTO) established as the replacement for GATT. WTO became the first international organ with a mechanism to resolve trade disputes between nations.

The world of officially supported export credits thus evolved in a world of scant regulation, and as competition between exporters hardened in the 1960's, govern-

1. Moravcik, 1989.
2. HSBC, 2015.

ments stepped in to the scene with long-term subsidised financing. Efforts to limit the extent of subsidies were blocked by the US, which had the benefit of low interest rates and thus were able to offer low interest loans to export transactions involving American companies. Only in 1975 did the OECD countries foster a 'gentleman agreement', the Consensus Arrangement, which laid down the basic terms and conditions for officially supported export credits as well as a mechanism for transparency.[3]

The creation of the Consensus Arrangement is, in itself, an interesting study of how international cooperation regimes can evolve (see Moravcsik, 1989). A plain version of the story would emphasise the changing incentives from the US side, as the oil shock and the costs of financing the Vietnam War caused interest rates to rise. This eroded the structural advantage that the US had in not having a strong international regime for regulating officially supported export credits.

The Consensus Arrangement has been amended many times since and has been successful in restricting the number of subsidies that governments provide to national exports. However, with the advent of China as a major exporting nation, the international regulation of officially supported export credits is proving less effective than in the three decades following the 1980's. China is not a member of the OECD and not subject to the rules of the Consensus Arrangement; a situation that China has exploited quite opportunistically. China has, in fact, several state sponsored institutions that are supporting exports from China, particularly to Emerging Markets and developing countries. For example, numerous infrastructure projects in Africa have benefitted from cheap Chinese financing.

Effect of the Financial Crisis

In the years preceding 2007, the private sector was doing a fantastic job of providing finance and allocating risk. It was a time of immense innovation in the financial sector. New techniques of risk management and slicing up tranches of sophisticated securities to target different investors' specific risk appetite had virtually eliminated the boom and bust character of earlier economic periods. The new era of the Great Moderation was characterised by high growth rates, virtually eliminated risks, and handsome rewards to bankers for their good deeds for society.

Of course, it was all soap bubbles and self-deception. The financial innovations believed to take manhood into a state of economic nirvana was in fact a monetary

---

3.   Moravscik, 1989.

doomsday machine that took the world to the brink of disaster, particularly the securities created on the basis of American sub-prime loans – these were a toxic creation that threatened to poison the groundwater of the global financial system. The advent of the crisis came in 2007, as lots of sub-prime loans reached the time of first repayment from the house-owning borrowers.[4] Many borrowers could not service their loans and the effects rippled through the mortgage market and into the securities markets, where subprime loans had been packaged and repackaged into more and more refined products.

In early 2008, the investment bank Bear Stearns – the biggest casualty of the crisis until that point – was bought out by JP Morgan at the instigation of the US treasury, who had provided a bailout loan of US 25 billion to avert Bear Stearns' collapse. In early September 2008, the US treasury bailed out mortgage lenders Fannie Mae and Freddie Mac, who at that point owned, or guaranteed about half of, the U.S.'s $12 trillion mortgage market, effectively nationalizing them. A few days later Bank of America bought investment bank Merrill Lynch, again at the instigation of the US treasury.

Already frightened about lacking liquidity, the financial markets turned to outright panic when Secretary of the Treasury Hank Paulson allowed another investment bank, Lehman Brothers, to collapse instead of being bailed out. The financial crisis was now a full-blown reality.

The effects of the financial crisis on the market for officially supported export credits is difficult to underestimate. Whereas prior to the crisis, markets believed that the private sector would do more and more export financing on its own – without public support – after the crisis, official Export Credit Agencies (ECAs) again became important players in the field, as seen from table 1.

New product offerings from ECAs proved important. In the years preceding the crisis, ECAs main offer was their guarantees against non-payment from foreign buyers of export goods. ECAs has expanded much in this traditional space, particularly in the direction of short-term credit guarantees, which is the natural arena for abovementioned private companies like Atradius, Euler Hermes, and Coface. However, these companies significantly withdrew their cover for export companies, and most ECAs stepped into the vacuum they thereby created.

Some ECAs also created two new product lines, which significantly increased their importance. One is the domestic financing programs, sometimes called working

---

4. To entice prospective house owners to take a loan despite their poor economic ability (and hence their 'sub-prime' status), many loans had an initial instalment-free – and sometimes even an interest-free – period in the beginning.

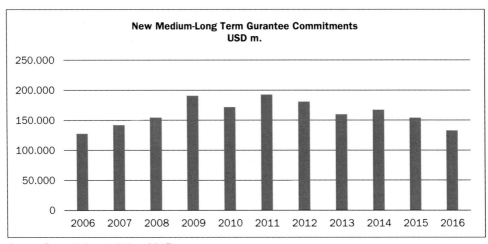

Source: Berne Union statistics, 2017

capital programs, which aims to help national companies get financing, whenever the domestic banking sector seems unable or unwilling to do the job. Another is the funding programs, which came as a response to the continued lack of long-term liquidity in the markets after the crisis. With such offering, the ECAs in question went from providing 'pure cover' (guarantees only) to also providing funding to banks and buyers of domestic goods.

Most ECAs and private trade insurance companies are members of the Berne Union, who takes its name from the Swiss city where it has been legally domiciled (though resides elsewhere) since it's inauguration in 1934.[5] Berne Union members are a significant part of international trade, providing guarantees for about 11% of world trade.[6] However, the bulk of Berne Union members' business is short-term credits (tenors of less than one year), which is primarily done by private market actors.

The realm of the officially supported export credits is the medium- & long-term business. In this field, the financial markets have regained their appetite and ability to finance export transactions. The tides are thus again turning away from officially supported export credits, whose combined volume of new Medium-Long term commitments peaked in 2011.

5. Moravczik, 1989.
6. Berne Union Yearbook 2017. When considering that a lot of cross-border trade is between subsidiaries within the same company (which is not insured), the Berne Union members' part in international trade is even higher.

The banks have repositioned themselves after the crisis and bolstered their balance sheet to observe the new regulation that came as a response to the financial crisis. Their capital has strengthened enough for them to start lending again – and the immense liquidity dispensed from central banks has created a significant 'hunt for yield' among all types of institutional investors, including pension funds, hedge funds, investment companies, etc. Some of the large infrastructure projects typically financed by ECAs (wind farms, power plants, ports, roads and the like) are interesting to such financial institutions as they are long-term investments with a stable return, something that is particularly interesting to pension funds.

The crisis has also caused the differences between ECAs to become more important. In some markets, the ability for an ECA to provide long term funding (liquidity) is an important competitive factor. Although many ECAs now have this ability, some ECAs do not. Another difference, strengthened by the crisis, is the one between ECAs backed by a AAA-rated state and those (often southern European) ECAs, whose backing government is lessor rated. When banks get guarantee cover from an AAA-rated ECA, they need not allocate any capital against losses on the loan. When the guarantee comes from a lessor rated ECA, the bank must allocate some capital against losses. This lessens the bank's return on equity a bit and makes them charge a slightly higher interest rate on the loan to the borrower. Loans covered by AAA-rated ECAs thus have lower interest rates and the exporters from AAA-rated countries have a competitive edge, whenever exporters from two different countries compete for the same contract.

Case Story, Lake Turkana Wind Power

Background

In the early 2000s, a group of hikers of Dutch descent tried to put up their tents at the shores of Lake Turkana in Northern Kenya. Much to their frustration, the tents kept blowing away in the constant winds. They were trying to camp in the valley between the foot slopes of Mt. Kulal and the south-eastern end of Lake Turkana. It turned out that the different and fluctuating temperatures between the lake and the desert hinterland generate strong, predictable wind streams. The local valley then functions as a funnel causing the wind streams to accelerate.

Wind measurements and power purchase agreement

The hikers saw a possibility for a wind farm and in 2006, the founding fathers (hikers) decided to formally investigate the wind resource at Lake Turkana. They installed the first of 10 wind measurement masts and appointed the German company DEWI to carry out wind measurement studies. As the first promising results from the wind measurement study came in, the decision was taken to carry out a full feasibility study for the project. In the meantime, the KP&P Africa B.V. consortium was formed, with the founding fathers and other Dutch and Kenyan companies and individuals. In 2008, negotiations began with the Kenya Power & Lighting Company Ltd, KPLC, on the first wind-power purchase agreement (PPA) in sub-Saharan Africa, which was finalized in May 2013.

Equity consortium

In 2010, KP&P entered into an equity agreement with Aldwych, and in 2011 Vestas (the Danish wind mill manufacturer), Norfund and IFU joined the equity group, followed by Finnfund and Sandpiper Ltd. in 2013. Today, these seven companies form the LTWP (Lake Turkana Wind Power) project company consortium.

Debt financing

In 2011, African Development Bank was given the assignment to structure the financing of the project, together with NedBank and Standard Bank. The project finally reached its financial close in December 2014. Other financiers involved in financing the project include European Investment Bank (EIB), FMO, DEG, Proparco and Triodos. However, the largest single risk taker in the project is the Danish Export Credit Agency, EKF, which is guaranteeing EUR 120 million to EIB. EKF's interest in supporting the project naturally comes through the 365 wind turbines supplied by Vestas.

The project is now fully constructed, able to provide 310MW of reliable, low cost energy to Kenya's national grid (approximately 18% of the country's installed capacity), which will be sold to KPLC over a 20-year period in accordance with the Power Purchase Agreement.

The extraordinary nature of the project is demonstrated by the fact that the majority of financing institutions participating in the project is DFIs (Development Finance Institutions) like AfDB, IFU, Norfund, FMO and DEG. However, the project could not have been realized without the substantial support of an ECA, in this case the Danish EKF.

Sources: https://ltwp.co.ke/ https://www.kppafrica.com/en

The search for yield among the private actors in the capital markets and the associated falling demand for officially supported export credits leaves ECAs in search of a new *raison d'etre*. As a corollary to the regulation of the unabashedly national subsidies, that officially supported export credits entailed in their early years, the justification for their continued (but regulated and subdued) existence became rooted in the concept of *guarantor of last resort.*[7] Just as a central bank in case of a bank run has the role of lender of last resort in order to maintain liquidity in the bank market, the activities of ECAs are justified by the existence of market gaps, in which only state-backed entities will operate. From this argument naturally follows that whenever the private market actors regain appetite for risk – as is the situation today – ECAs should gracefully withdraw from the market, as the gaps are no longer so prominent.

This, however, might run counter to the wishes of the ECAs themselves, now adjusted to the glory of the limelight in the financial markets. Few organizations are eager to see their activity decline – and the ECAs might also have become too ingrained in the fabric of financial markets to simply wither in light of private actors' increased willingness to provide finance and insurance to the trade credit market. The rapidly growing supply of private trade credit reinsurance is very willing to receive business from ECAs. And although the ECAs use the private reinsurance market to relieve themselves of specific risks, their portfolios typically remain too concentrated, and of too long tenor, to appear appetizing to any private insurer or bank.[8]

Some transactions are simply too risky in the eyes of the private market actors, particularly when there is a combination of new technologies making their entry into new markets. An example of this is Africa's largest wind farm at Lake Turkana (see box), which needed the support of ECAs and other public sources of finance to become a reality.

References

Ascari, R. (2007). 'Is Export Credit Agency a Misnomer? The ECA Response to a Changing World'. Working Paper No. 02. Gruppo SACE.

Auboin, M. (2009). Boosting the Availability of Trade Finance in the Current Crisis: Background Analysis for a Substantial G20 Package. CEPR.

Hsbc (2015). 'Trade Winds: shaping the future of international business', HSBC 2015.

Klasen, A. (2011). *'The Role of Export Credit Agencies in Global Trade'*, Global Policy Volume 2. Issue 2. May 2011, London School of Economics and Political Science and John Wiley & Sons Ltd. pp. 220-222.

Moravcsik, A. (1989). 'Disciplining Trade Finance – the OECD Trade Export Arrangement', International Organization, Volume 43, Issue 1; January 1989, pp. 173-205.

Vesteri, T. (2017). 'Foreword from the Berne Union President', in Berne Union (ed.), Berne Union Yearbook 2017. London: TXF, pp. 11-15.

7. Klasen, 2011.
8. Ascari, 2007.

Foreign Direct Investment in Developing Countries:

Engine of Development or Tool of Exploitation?

By Michael W. Hansen and Henrik Gundelach, Center for Business and Development Studies CBS

Foreign Direct Investment in Developing Countries
Introduction

When multinational corporations (MNCs) invest to get control of activities in a foreign location it is called foreign direct investment (FDI). Over the last few decades, FDI has grown with much faster rates than GDP and trade. Indeed, rather than trade, which propelled previous incidences of internationalization, FDI is the key driver of the current internationalization.

What is foreign direct investment (FDI)?

FDI is investment made to acquire a lasting interest in an economy other than that of the investor, the investor's purpose being to have an effective voice in the management of the enterprise

FDI can be financed through capital transfers, loans or repatriation of profits. Value of technology, services or inputs are considered FDI.

Measured by national banks' balance of payment statistics. In practice defined as investments where the foreign investor has at least 10% (25% in some countries) ownership.

For developing countries, FDI is one of the key elements in industrial development strategy. FDI may hold part of the answer to many of the development challenges facing developing countries, e.g. how to get hold of advanced technology and knowledge, how to access products and services that are needed to solve development problems, or how to gain access to foreign markets. FDI by very large MNCs in particular is also sometimes a cause of concern for developing countries. This is due to MNCs' superior resources and market positions which may threaten local industries, as well as MNCs' ability to leverage resources across borders which may potentially allow them to evade government control.

This chapter will explore how FDI is related to development and how developing countries are seeking to extract developmental rents from FDI.

The changing Landscape of FDI

During the 20 years leading up to the 2008 financial crises, FDI was expanding rapidly relative to economies and trade. While FDI growth has stagnated since then, foreign investors keep on investing at very high levels so that the accumulated value of FDI made by the more than 60,000 MNCs exceeds $25 trillion. On top of the activities under MNC ownership control, MNCs have, during the past 20 years, increasingly complemented FDI with non-equity means of internationalization such as alliances and networks, to such an extent that observers label the current stage of internationalization as 'alliance capitalism'. Networks and alliances are fostered, partly to access assets of other firms (e.g. local market knowledge, unique technological capabilities, distribution networks, etc.), and partly to leverage their own advantages and assets more effectively.

What is a Developing Country?

According to the OECD, countries that are eligible for receiving 'Overseas Development Assistance (ODA)' are designated as 'Developing Countries'.

The World Bank classifies countries based on GNI income per capita, and developing countries are considered to be the group of 'Low and Middle Income Countries' according to this classification.

A large proportion of FDI is being directed towards developing countries, and between 40 and 50% of FDI has in recent years been invested in developing countries (see Figure 1), up from 20 to 30% a decade ago. This is partly a consequence of MNCs from developed countries seeking access to markets and resources in developing countries, and partly a consequence of MNCs from developing countries increasing-

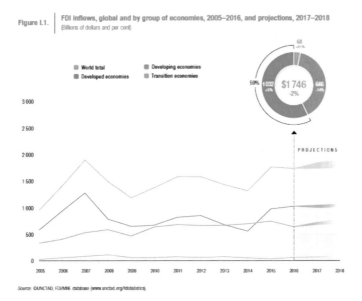

Figure I.1. FDI inflows, global and by group of economies, 2005–2016, and projections, 2017–2018
(Billions of dollars and per cent)

Source: OUNCTAD, FDI/MNE database (www.unctad.org/fdistatistics).

ly investing in other developing countries. Hence, where FDI traditionally was undertaken by MNCs located in developed countries, developing countries themselves are now large players in FDI, accounting for app. 40% of global FDI. The growing importance of developing countries in FDI is a logical consequence of the change in the gravity of global economic activity toward developing countries.

The role of MNCs in global economic activity is immense. MNCs account for 25% of global GDP and their app 500,000 subsidiaries account for 10% of global GDP. On the top 100 list of the world's largest economies, 25 are MNCs. While MNCs overall have most of their activity in their home countries, the share of foreign activities is increasing, especially MNCs headquartered in countries with small home markets – such as Switzerland or Denmark. These have very high transnationalization index (TNI) scores in comparison to MNCs in large countries and often 80+% of their activities will take place outside their home country.

It is estimated that MNCs employ more than 75 million people in their foreign subsidiaries and even more people at local firms providing inputs to the MNC subsidiary. MNCs are essentially extremely effective vehicles for transferring and integrating people, knowledge and skills across borders: MNCs move employees between their subsidiaries, either by sending expatriates abroad or by exchanging talent between subsidiaries. MNCs are also key players in organizing knowledge production at an international scale; 80% of civil Research & Development (R&D) takes place in MNCs and MNCs hold the bulk of patents and trademarks in the world.

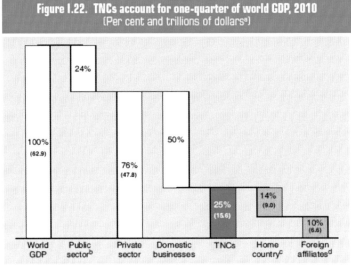

Figure I.22. TNCs account for one-quarter of world GDP, 2010
(Per cent and trillions of dollars[a])

Source: UNCTAD.
[a] Current prices, current exchange rates.
[b] ISIC L, M, N, Q, X, 92, P (Public administration, Defence, Social security, Health,
   Sanitation, Community services, Private household employment).
[c] As estimated by the weighted average size of home economies.
[d] Table I.5 in this report.

Furthermore, MNCs are key to organizing international trade. One-third of all trade is MNC internal and another third is between MNCs and their foreign alliance partners.

FDI as an Engine of Development

Given the assets and resources of MNCs and their key role in organizing cross border economic activity, it is not surprising that developing countries are focusing on how to extract development benefits from FDI.

Typically, developing countries are short on capital to fund development projects and FDI can here provide an important source of development finance. In fact, FDI is the most important source of development finance for developing countries overall, dwarfing official development assistance (ODA), portfolio investments (investments that are not aimed at gaining management control of foreign activities) and remittances. As FDI is typically invested in buildings and equipment, it is relatively sticky compared to portfolio investments in e.g. shares. Hence, in times of balance-of-payment crises, FDI will tend to stabilize rather than destabilize the economy.

Figure I.12. | External sources of finance for developing economies, 2007–2016 (Billions of dollars)

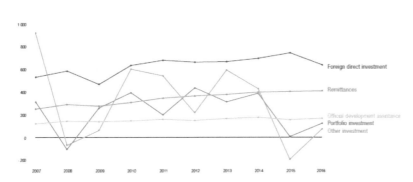

Source: OUNCTAD, based on data from IMF (for portfolio and other investment), from the UNCTAD FDI/MNE database (for FDI inflows), from the Organization for Economic Cooperation and Development (for ODA) and from the World Bank (for remittances)

Note: Other investment includes loans among non affiliated enterprises.

Even if FDI is highly unevenly distributed among developing countries – app. two-thirds of developing country FDI is in Asia and more than 95% goes to the middle income developing countries – FDI often play very important roles even in the least developed countries when measured in relation to the size of the local economy.

The development role of FDI cannot be measured in terms of capital alone. In addition to capital, FDI is also a bundle of resources and assets, such as technology, skills, patents, networks, people, etc. All these assets and resources may be utilized by developing countries and contribute to job creation and upgrading of the domestic industrial capacity. While such assets in some instance could have been acquired by other means than FDI (e.g. through imports of equipment, licenses, reverse engineering, franchising, etc.), many of them are intangibles (e.g. distribution networks, organizational capabilities and processes, experience, etc.) and therefore difficult to acquire in the market. Other assets, such as patents and trademarks may be unob-

Table I.10. UNCTAD's FDI Contribution Index, by host region, 2009[a] (Percentage shares in each variable's total for the region)							
Region/economy	Value added	Employment	Exports	Tax revenue	Wages and salaries	R&D expenditures	Capital expenditures
Total world							
Developed countries	12.7	7.5	19.3	13.9	14.6	24.2	10.5
Developing economies	12.2	7.9	17.3	14.6	15.4	24.1	11.6
Africa	21.7	7.3	..	..	21.7	37.2	18.4
East and South-East Asia	10.5	9.9	30.9	7.7	8.9	22.5	6.2
South Asia	10.3	6.1	..	..	16.0	..	3.8
West Asia	16.8	5.5	1.9	..	15.0	..	3.8
Latin America and the Caribbean	15.9	6.0	17.9	18.9	16.0	35.0	14.8
Transition economies	21.7	3.0	..	..	11.2	15.4	25.7

Source: UNCTAD; for further information on data and methodology, see www.unctad.org/wir.
[a] Or latest year available.
Note: Data from economies not listed in the FDI Contribution Index (because they do not cover at least four of the seven variables), are included in these calculations.

tainable due to IPR protection, or they may be impossible to organize through arm's-length processes (insourcing) due to quality and control issues. Hence, a key point about MNCs and development is that MNCs potentially make assets and resources available that would not otherwise – or only under great costs – be available to developing countries. Therefore, if host countries are to access advanced production technology, technical and managerial skills and knowledge, foreign export markets, or financial capital, they often need the presence of MNCs. Consequently, we often see FDI in developing countries in sectors where local assets cannot be exploited (e.g. resource extraction), in sectors where there is high capital intensity (e.g. infrastructure and energy), or in sectors where there are large entry barriers in export markets (e.g. food stuffs, textile and garments or electronics).

As mentioned, a defining characteristic of the modern MNC is its networked nature. Hence, MNCs cultivate linkages to other firms in order to leverage more effectively their own advantages and to access complementary assets. In relation to developing countries, local linkages are particularly important as MNCs need such linkages to circumvent their liabilities of foreignness (i.e. additional costs of foreign firms compared to local firms), to tap into local firm cost advantages, or to comply with regulatory requirements of local content stipulations. As a consequence, a MNC subsidiary will often be the tip of the iceberg in terms of development impact; typically for each job created at the MNC subsidiary, one to two jobs will be created at local linkage partners.

What are spillovers and linkages?

Linkages are interfirm relations beyond pure market transactions. An organizational form where formal and informal collaborative exchanges between legally independent firms, where material and immaterial resources are transferred, and/or practices shared and transmitted

Spillovers are (positive) unintended side effects of market transactions (externalities), i.e. an effect. Spillovers occur 'when the efficiency of local firms improves as a result of foreign entry, and the foreigner does not internalize the benefits', and/or 'when local firms benefit from the MNC affiliates' superior knowledge of product or process technologies or markets, without incurring a cost that exhausts the whole gain from the improvement' (Kokko, 2003).

Spillovers and linkages are closely related. Hence, the presence of linkages makes spillovers (e.g. learning) more likely.

Another indirect effect of FDI is the so-called spillovers, i.e. unintended effects on unrelated local firms. As a point of departure, a MNC will not share its assets with local firms and when it does, it will typically be part of a contractual arrangement.

However, some assets cannot be fully controlled in-house or though contracts and will tend to diffuse to local firms: former MNC employees may use the skills acquired in other firms; local firms may imitate the organizational and technological practices of MNCs; MNCs' standards may become de facto or de jure industry standards; or MNCs may infuse more competition into local industries. These spillovers may be the most important and lasting effect of FDI on developing countries.

Some effects of FDI derive from the production of goods and services, others from the provision of goods and services. The latter type of effects may be especially important to developing countries: MNCs will bring in goods and services that it would otherwise be difficult to acquire. A case in point is energy production, where MNCs may be able to organize the often extremely costly and technologically and organizationally complex provision of energy services. Another example is that MNCs may adopt Base of the Pyramid (BoP) strategies where they introduce products and services that are specifically tailored to meet the needs of the poor, e.g. by adapting distribution and packaging to the purchasing power and preferences of the poor, or by developing new products and services that solve development challenges.

FDI and poverty: Bottom-of-the-pyramid strategies

In 2002, renowned business economist Prahalad introduced the term Bottom of the Pyramid into MNC business strategy. His argument was that MNCs can make money by re-designing their strategies to cater to the poor. One example he gave was Hindustan Lever (Unilever's Indian subsidiary) which successfully sold detergents and soap to the poor in rural India by packaging in small batches and by setting up a special distribution infrastructure with small moms and pops outlets.

While Prahalad's idea has generated huge interest, it has also been criticised both for the normative aspects of the BoP strategy (making money from the poor) as well as for the lack of actual examples of BoP strategies in MNCs.

But there may also be a gloomier side to FDI seen from the perspective of developing countries. As argued, FDI is potentially generating development due to their superior technology and organization and their global presence. However, those advantages also carry a risk for developing countries. In particular, MNCs may crowd out local industries and obtain local market dominance. Part of the discontent with FDI originates from the fear of economic decline in the host countries arising from crowding out many local firms and suffocating domestic technological development. Similarly, domestic firms may suffer profit losses as MNCs capture their market shares from them. If the profit losses are severe, the domestic firms may close down completely leading to welfare losses in the host economy. Crowding out domestic investment is also detested for some non-economic reasons such as the potential loss of national sovereignty. As the defining characteristic of FDI is capital transfer *with* controlling ownership, FDI essentially implies that host countries surrender control over parts of their economy and that many essential activities will be coordinated not only from the host country, but also from a headquarters in a foreign country.

FDI in African extractives: Enclaves or new development opportunity?

Traditionally, extractive FDI in Africa has been seen as the enclave economy par excellence, moving in with fully integrated value chains, extracting resources and exporting them as commodities having virtually no linkages to the local economy. However, new opportunities for promoting linkages are offered by changing business strategies of local African enterprises as well as foreign multinational corporations (MNCs). MNCs in extractives are increasingly seeking local linkages as part of their efficiency, risk and asset seeking strategies and linkage programmes are becoming integral elements in many MNCs' corporate social responsibility (CSR) activities. At the same time, local African enterprises are eager to, and are increasingly capable of, linking up to the foreign investors in order to expand their activities and acquire technology, skills and market access. The changing strategies of MNCs and the improving capabilities of African enterprises offer new opportunities for governments and donors to mobilize extractive FDI for development goals.

The MNCs reluctance to share their ownership specific advantages will prevent local producers from climbing up the ladder and local producers may be stuck in low value-added activities in global value chains. In some instances, especially in extractive sectors, MNCs may form enclaves with little spillover into the host economy. This is partly a consequence of the huge technology gap that often exists between MNCs and local industries, and partly that local industries lack the absorptive capacity to pick up and learn from the MNCs. MNCs may hold solutions to problems in more technologically advanced developing countries and more advanced segments of economies, but for the poorest countries and for the poor, there may be little connection or spillover. In some cases, MNCs interact with political systems in un-ethical ways where MNCs, in return for concessions, permits and approvals, pay facility payments or even engage in corruption with local politicians and administrative officers.

Government Strategies toward FDI

Based on the huge positive and negative potential of FDI, it is no wonder that FDI policy is key to any economic development strategy around the developing world. Historically, developing countries have adopted different approaches to steer FDI. In the early post-colonial period in the 1950s and '60s, host countries wanted to gain control over their economies, and intervention focused on nationalization and restriction of FDI. Most developing countries, with notable exceptions such as Singapore and Malaysia, adopted restrictive approaches to FDI, where FDI was either prohibited, only allowed if there was local ownership, or with stringent performance requirements such as export and local content requirements. During the 1980s and '90s, balance of payment crises and increasingly evident negative side effects of restrictive approaches to FDI forced many developing countries - often with the aid of International Monetary Fund and the World Bank - to open up to foreign investors. The bargaining position of the developing countries was often weak, and economies were liberalized without sufficient safeguards for local industries. In some countries, especially in Africa, this lead to undesirable side-effects, e.g. virtual de-industrialization and import-dependency. From the 2000s onwards, the focus of developing countries in relation to FDI has increasingly been on strategic targeting and selection. On the one hand this includes embracing FDI as a key ingredient in industrial development strategy, while on the other maintaining a managed approach to FDI by only gradually opening of sectors and imposing local content and local ownership requirements in a measured manner.

IFU, the Danish Investment fund for developing countries

FDI is not only sought harnessed for development in host countries. Most developed countries have investment promotion programmes as part of their development programmes. One of the largest such investment funds is Danish IFU. This organization is aimed at promoting sustainable development through equity investment. It assists Danish investment in developing countries through providing equity and loans as well as by providing advice. The fund has become a key player in Danish FDI and it is estimated that it participates in between one-quarter and one-third of Danish FDI.

Most recently, developed and developing countries are connecting FDI to development assistance. The United Nations Millennium Declaration from 2000 highlighted an international concern about the developing countries' difficulties in obtaining necessary finance for their sustained development. The world's leaders held their first International Conference on Financing for Development in Mexico in 2002. The result of the conference was a turning point in the approach to development cooperation, as it declared that 'Private international capital flows, particularly foreign direct investment, along with international financial stability, are vital complements to national and international development efforts. Foreign direct investment contributes toward financing sustained economic growth over the long term'. Several world leaders stressed a need for domestic policies to increase the benefits of FDI. Despite concerns among both politicians and NGOs about an uneven distribution of FDI, the important role of FDI in creating a global framework for financing development was again emphasized at the third International Conference on Financing for Development in Addis Ababa in 2015. Later in 2015 the Sustainable Development Goals (SDGs) were adopted at the United Nation General Assembly and the world leaders wanted to establish 'a holistic and forward-looking framework' for their implementation. The scene was set for a growing interest in combining traditional state-financed Overseas Development Assistance and private investments, and in the process of implementing the SDGs, so-called 'blended finance' has become an important device.

Development Finance Institutions (DFIs)

During the aftermath of World War II, the allied in North America and Western Europe identified a global strategic role for providing financial aid to developing countries. The aid was almost entirely through tax-financed ODA, such as loans and grants given to governments and NGOs. This was, however, also the time when a new breed of government backed investment banks were established as so-called Development Finance Institutions to support private sector investments under difficult conditions in developing countries. The idea that private firms could profit from development aid was naturally controversial in parts of the political spectrum, but successful private sector development projects as well as a mounting pressure on public finances world-wide gave the idea increased credence.

Development Finance Institutions (DFIs) are specialized development banks that are usually majority owned by national governments. DFIs can be bilateral, serving to implement their government's foreign development and cooperation policy, or multilateral, acting as private sector arms of International Finance Institutions (IFIs).

CDC Group of the United Kingdom (formerly the Commonwealth Development Corporation) was established in 1948 with a mission to 'do good without losing money', and the German Investment and Development Company (DEG) is among the largest in the world. Denmark established its Investment Fund for Developing Countries (IFU) in 1967 to offer risk capital and advisory services to firms wishing to invest in developing countries. The largest global multilateral development institution is International Finance Corporation (IFC), which is a part of the World Bank and is focused exclusively on investments in the private sector in developing countries.

Future Challenges

Governments around the world have discovered the potential of FDI and are adopting more strategic approaches to FDI where focus is on FDI selection rather than FDI promotion. These more assertive approaches are inspired by the Asian economies' and especially China's hands-on approach to manage FDI. But uncritically supplanting the experience of Asian countries with strong states to countries with weak states, as is the case in much of the developing world, will not work. Any strategy to extract the benefits of FDI must take into account the country's governance capacity as well as the absorptive capacity of the local industry.

At the end of the day it can be questioned whether national approaches to management of FDI will suffice. There is a real risk that countries, in their efforts to attract FDI, will undermine each other's efforts and embark on a race-to-the-bottom in terms of taxation, salaries and social and environmental standards. Hence, there is a need for governments to coordinate their activities internationally. Currently, however, there is no global governance architecture for FDI similar to what exists in the trade field and prospects for such an architecture to be established are bleak. In this governance vacuum, governments must look for innovative approaches to steer the activities of MNCs, e.g. by fostering development partnerships such as seen in the SDG field, by adopting innovative financial mechanisms such as blended finance instruments, or by encouraging MNCs to internalize development objectives in their strategies such as is the case with MNCs pursuing BoP strategies.

Globalisation has Changed the Rules of The Danish Labour Market

By Søren V. Kristensen, Macro Economist at Sydbank

In the course of the last 50 years, the globalisation process of the world has dramatically increased. The increasing globalisation has a considerable impact on the economy as well as society at large in many countries. Denmark is no exception in that regard. Increasing globalisation and its effects can be witnessed in many aspects of the Danish economy. For instance, in the labour market where globalisation materialises as a large increase in the number of foreign workers in the labour force and increased competition from companies around the globe.

Denmark is focused on exploiting the labour market benefits of globalisation

Denmark has sought, in several ways, to exploit the possibilities that globalisation offers in regards to the labour market. An important factor in this respect is Denmark's membership of the European Union (EU) and access to the so-called single market where member countries can trade without any transaction costs. Furthermore, the single market allows free movement of labour within the EU. This has played a major role in the Danish labour market in the last decade. Especially after the EU was expanded in 2004 and 2007 where several Eastern European countries joined the EU. In addition, Denmark has implemented several internal measures to ease the barrier of entry into the Danish labour market for foreign workers. These include special visa rules and changes to the tax system in order to attract foreign workers to the Danish labour market. The tax measures are primarily targeted at highly-skilled foreign workers.

Denmark's membership of the EU, the tax and visa rules combined with the general globalisation process, have no doubt increased the number of foreigners in the Danish labour market. In the course of the last two decades, the total number of immigrants in Denmark has doubled and around 10 percent of the total population is now immigrants. They tend to be relatively young workers, aged 25 to 44, that enter the Danish labour force, and in terms of both wages and industries, they are relatively well distributed, though they are particularly well represented in the service sector.

Labour market immigration generates a demand for regulation

The immigration into a both unionized and regulated labour market such as the Danish one generates a strong demand for enforcement of the regulation. In Denmark it is important to ensure that foreign workers are paid and treated in compliance with the Danish labour union agreements, otherwise firms in some sectors will be able to attract foreign workers at wages far below the Danish minimum wage level, as such wages will still be higher than what the workers would be able to earn in their home country. This will put immense pressure on Danish workers who will be subject to unfair competition. At the same time foreign workers will have to get by on wages barely sufficient to live on in Denmark. The phenomenon is usually referred to as social dumping. Due to an intense focus from politicians and labour unions this is not a major problem in the Danish labour market.

The number of immigrants is highly dependent on the current labour market situation

The Danish experience shows that the immigration of foreign workers is largely dependent on the situation of the labour market in Denmark. During the years 2005 to 2007, the number of foreign workers in the Danish labour force almost doubled. A similar development is observable from 2013 and until now (autumn 2017) where the workforce has been joined by a large number of foreigners. Conversely, experience shows that during recessions foreigners tend to leave again as their job chances deteriorate. As a result, it seems that the Danish labour market is becoming even more flexible. This diminishes the risk of an overheated labour market and thereby extends the lives of economic booms in Denmark. The Danish evidence is quite clear on this point – increased immigration plays an important role in economic booms and has lowered the risk of an overheating of the Danish labour market.

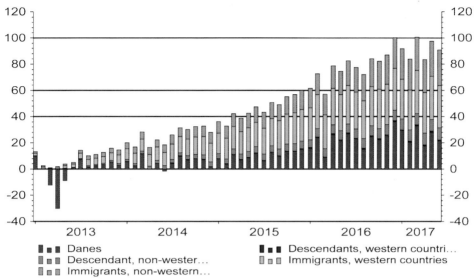

Danes
Descendant, non-wester...
Immigrants, non-western...
Descendants, western countri...
Immigrants, western countries

Kilde: Thomson Reuters Datastream, Jobindsats og egne beregniniger

Immigrants have lifted the productivity level in Denmark

The foreigners in the labour force have a great potential impact on the native members of the labour force. They can affect the level of both wages and employment of native workers. Furthermore, the increased recruiting possibilities affect productivity and thereby the wage level and wealth of native workers. Empirical evidence also points to the fact that foreigners have impacted the labour market situation for native workers.

In terms of productivity immigrants can increase the productivity level through several channels. The obvious channel for improved productivity through immigration is the possibility that foreign workers bring new skills to the Danish labour market. Another source of an increase in productivity could be that immigrants complement the Danish workforce in a way that increases the general productivity level. In Denmark it could be through the import of low-skilled workers that complement the generally highly skilled Danish labour force so that productivity increases for both parties. Empirical evidence indicates that immigrants have lifted the level of productivity in Denmark. This also means that the internationalisation of the workforce has contributed to an increase in the general level of wealth in Denmark.

The evidence on wages and employment is ambiguous

This will generally lead to higher wages for immigrants as well as natives in the labour force. There are, however, other more direct and short-term effects on the wage level of natives in the workforce. In the short term, immigration will result in a downward wage pressure due to the increased supply of labour. Evidence suggests that the effect on the wage level of native Danish workers has, however, been somewhat asymmetric. Since immigrants have been mostly unskilled workers going into the service sector, native Danes working in this part of the economy have been affected the most. Most evidence shows that immigration typically means subdued wage growth for low-skilled workers whereas high-skilled workers actually experience higher wage growth. On the other hand, prices in the service sector in particular are also subdued, which benefits all Danes, even though the benefit is greatest for those who consume many services. In the long term, firms will tend to restore the capital/labour ratio and hence the wage effects will tend to vanish.

Naturally, immigration also affects the employment level of the native workers. The mechanism is quite clear. The increased supply of potential labour will raise the bar for entering the labour market. This will potentially push some of the natives out of the labour market. As one would expect, most studies of the Danish labour market suggest that the employment rate of low-skilled native Danish workers has been negatively affected while there is no significant effect on the employment rate of high-skilled workers.

In conclusion, native Danes in the labour market feel the effects of globalisation in several ways. From a macro perspective this also transforms into effects on the general labour market and thereby the entire economy. As mentioned one of the most important factors is that globalisation – and thereby the increased recruiting possibilities – diminishes the risk of an overheating of the Danish labour market. So even in a situation of full employment, wage growth will not necessarily speed up. In other words, the domestic Phillips curve has flattened considerably during the last decade. Therefore, it is fair to say that globalisation has changed the rules of the Danish labour market.

The increasing number of immigrants is not the only factor causing the flattening of the Phillips curve. It is also affected by the increase in international competition stemming from globalisation. Consumers can compare prices around the globe and that makes it difficult to raise wages despite pressure in the domestic labour market. This transforms into subdued wage growth, not only in Denmark but also in many other countries around the globe. As a result, inflation remains low in Denmark as well as in many other countries and partly due to low inflation interest rates are at record low levels in many countries.

To sum up, globalisation has a great impact on the Danish labour market and the economy in general. It makes the labour market less vulnerable to overheating but it also makes it harder for some groups of native Danish workers to find a job. Moreover, globalisation puts downward pressure on interest rates and the interest rate level in Denmark is now among the lowest in the world.

Bibliography

Acemoglu, Daron and James A. Robinson (2012). *Why Nations Fail*, Crown Publishers.

Andersen, Torben M., Jan Bentzen, Svend E. Hougaard Jensen, Valdemar Smith, Niels Westergaard-Nielsen (2017). *The Danish Economy in a Global Context*, Copenhagen: DJØF Publishing.

Baldwin, Richard (2006). *Globalisation: The Great Unbundling(s)*. Prime Ministers Office. Finland.

Bonvillian, William B. (2017). *U.S. Manufacturing Decline and the Rise of New Production Innovation Paradigms – OECD*. Oecd.org. N. p., 2017. Web. 27 May 2017.

Bordo, Michael D. (2002). 'Globalization in Historical Perspective', *Business Economics*.

Borio, Claudio and Piti Disyatat, BIS Working Papers, No. 346, *Global Imbalances and the Financial Crisis: Link or No Link?* Bank for International Settlements, May 2011.

Broome, André (2014). *Issues and Actors in the Global Political Economy*. Basingstoke: Palgrave Macmillan.

Danmarks Nationalbank (2016). Globale værdikæder, Kvartalsoversigt, 1. kvartal 2016.

Danmarks Nationalbank (1993). Dansk pengehistorie 1960-1990.

Dicken, Peter (2015). *Global Shifts*, 7th Edition, SAGE.

Dieckheuer, Gustav (2001). *Internationale Wirtschaftsbeziehungen*. München: Oldenbourg.

Giddens, Anthony (1990). *The Consequences of Modernity*. Polity Press/Blackwell Publishing.

Gilpin, Robert (2001). *Global Political Economy: Understanding the International Economic Order*. Princeton: Princeton University Press.

Hidalgo, C.A, B. Klinger, A.-L. Barabási, R. Hausmann (2007). The Product Space Conditions the Development of Nations, *Science*.

Justesen, Mogens K. (2010). 'Political Dilemmas and the Institutional Foundation of Economic Development', *World Political Science Review*, 6 (1).

Katzenstein, P.J. (1985). *Small States in World Markets: Industrial Policy in Europe*. Ithaca NY: Cornell University Press.

Kapstein, E.B. (2000). Winners and Losers in the Global Economy. *International Organization*, 54(2).

Keohane, Robert (1984). *After Hegemony: Cooperation and Discord in the World Political Economy*. Princeton: Princeton University Press.

Keynes, John M. *Collected Works*, Vol. XXV. Cambridge: University Press.

Keynes, John M. (1920). *The Economic Consequences of the Peace*. Harcourt, Brace and Howe.

Krugman, P., Maurice Obstfeld and Melitz, M. (2015). *International Economics*. 10th Edition, Harlow: Pearson.

Kwon, R. (2012). Hegemonic Stability, World Cultural Diffusion, and Trade Globalization 1. *Sociological Forum*, 27(2), 324-347.

Mankiw, N. Gregory and Mark P. Taylor (2014). *Macroeconomics*. 2nd Edition, Worth Publishers.

McKinsey Global Institute (2017). *The New Dynamics of Financial Globalisation*, August.

Mehmet, Ozay (1999). *Westernizing the third world: the Euro centricity of economic development theories*. London: Routledge.

MIT, Krugman, Ricardo: http://web.mit.edu/krugman/www/ricardo.htm

O'Rourke, Kevin (2009). 'Politics and Trade: Lessons from Past Globalisations', Bruegel.

OECD (2018). *FDI in Figures*, April.

Pedersen, Ove Kaj (2011). *Konkurrencestaten*. Copenhagen: Hans Reitzel.

Porter, Michael (1990). 'The Competitive Advantages of Nations'. *Harvard Business Review*, March-April.

Rasumussen, Poul Nyrop (2007). *The Danish Model of 'Flexicurity'*. AARP International Perspectives (1ˢᵗ April).

Ravenhill, John (2014). *Global Political Economy*. 4ᵗʰ Edition. Oxford: Oxford University Press.

Rodrik, Dani (2003). *In Search of Prosperity: Analytic Narratives on Economic Growth*. Princeton University.

Salvatore, Dominick. Import Penetration, Exchange Rates, And Protectionism In The United States. *Journal of Policy Modeling* 9.1 (1987): 125-141. Web.

Salvatore, Dominick (2011). *International economics: trade and finance*. Hoboken: Wiley.

Schumacher, Reinhard. (2012). 'Adam Smith's theory of absolute advantage and the use of doxography in the history of economics'. *Erasmus Journal for Philosophy and Economics*, 5(2), 54-80. Online reference: http://ejpe.org/pdf/5-2-art-3.pdf

Smith, Adam (1976 [1776]). 'An inquiry into the nature and causes of the wealth of nations [WN]'. In R.H. Campbell, and A.S. Skinner (eds) *The Glasgow edition of the works and correspondence of Adam Smith*, Vol. 2. Oxford: Oxford University Press.

United Nations, Commission of Experts on Reforms on the International Monetary and Financial System, *Recommendations*. Sixty-third session, Agenda Item 48, 19 March. 2009, http://www.un.org/ga/president/63/letters/recommendationExperts200309

Williamson, Jeffrey G. *Winners and Losers Over Two Centuries of globalization*. NBER working paper 9161, 2002.

WN: See *Smith, Adam*.

Zhang, Wei-Bin (2008). *International trade theory: capital, knowledge, economic structure, money, and prices over time*. Berlin: Springer.

Index